D0252223

East Bay Bike Trails

Road and Mountain Bicycle Rides
through Alameda and Contra Costa Counties

by
Conrad J. Boisvert

Penngrove Publications
P.O. Box 1017
Penngrove, CA 94951
(707) 795-8911

For Judy, Charles and Stephen,
my most important creations

Library of Congress Catalog Card Number 92-80086
International Standard Book Number 0-9621694-4-7

Cover photograph by Jeff Dooley
Taken on Nimitz Way in Tilden Park, Berkeley
Cyclists: Conrad Boisvert and Jean Newton

Photographs in the book were taken by Conrad Boisvert

Printed in the United States of America
Lithocraft, Inc.
424 Aviation Boulevard
Santa Rosa, California

First printing, April 1992

𝓟enngrove Publications
P.O. Box 1017
Penngrove, CA 94951
(707) 795-8911

TABLE OF CONTENTS

ACKNOWLEDGMENTS

My appreciation to the many people who supported me in this book begins with my family. Thanks to my mother for her continuing encouragement and to my children, Judy, Charles and Stephen, for their genuine interest.

For her warmth, her love, and her critical eye as a fellow writer, I am deeply indebted to Jean Newton. The patience and companionship of my many cycling buddies, including Kathy Picard, Robert Warman, Holly Quittman, Bob Godwin, Klaus Schumann, Kellie Reed and the entire cycling gang at the Decathlon Club, are greatly appreciated.Carl Hartshorn, for his ongoing help on computer issues, also deserves my sincere thanks.

As was the case in our past efforts together, Phyllis Neumann has again demonstrated great patience and professionalism in handling the many problems routinely encountered in publishing a book of this kind. Finally, thanks to Jeff Dooley for his fine cover photograph and to Linda Cardone for her excellent editing.

Nimitz Way in Tilden Park

EXPLORE THE EAST BAY BY BIKE

If the ideal geographical area for cycling were to have been designed by a human, instead of by Mother Nature, it would most certainly look a lot like the San Francisco Bay Area. Blessed with a near-perfect climate, gifted with some of the most beautiful mountain ranges and forests, and punctuated by the presence of one of the most spectacular bays in the world, the Bay Area brings the joy of cycling to its apex. The East Bay, sheltered somewhat by distance from coastal fog and ocean winds common on the Peninsula, is often warmer and has some of the most remote country roads in the entire Bay Area.

Extending from the Carquinez Strait in the north to Fremont and Milpitas in the south, and from San Francisco Bay in the west to the Delta in the east, the East Bay encompasses the counties of Alameda, Contra Costa and parts of Santa Clara. The wide variety of scenery afforded by the East Bay is evident when contrasting the heavily wooded hills above Oakland and Berkeley, the drama of dominant Mount Diablo in Danville, the orchards and farms around Brentwood, the unique and eerie windmills in the Altamont Pass in Livermore and the bay wetlands around Newark.

The abundance of little known country roads with minimal car traffic stands in sharp contrast to the much better known freeways and busy city streets of the heavily populated cities and towns of the East Bay. While cycling in residential neighborhoods is usually the common thing to do, the truly best rides can only be experienced by transporting bikes to other, more remote, places.

The East Bay is also quite rich with opportunities for off-road riding. One of the finest examples of a well-managed open space plan is the East Bay Regional Park District, with 47 parks under its jurisdiction, most with at least some biking trails. The District also includes 11 regional trails, each of which consists of a paved or gravel path for use by pedestrians, runners, equestrians and cyclists. Not to be outdone, Mount Diablo State Park encompasses the single largest park area in the East Bay, with many miles of trails over some very challenging terrain for mountain bike riders of all abilities.

East Bay Bike Trails is intended for the recreational cyclist, with a wide variety of carefully planned rides offering suitable challenge for any ability level. Each area of the East Bay is represented, with the emphasis placed upon scenery, points of interest and minimum car traffic. The time is right, the challenge is before you — get on your bike and enjoy the sights of the East Bay.

REGIONS OF THE EAST BAY

Northern Region: The Carquinez Strait and Lafayette

A dominant feature of the northern section of the East Bay is the Carquinez Strait, accented by the aptly named road, Carquinez Scenic Drive, running along the shoreline crest overlooking the Strait. The waterway is the essential link between the Sacramento River Delta and San Francisco Bay and most days find it busy with cargo traffic. The rest of the region includes the countryside surrounding San Pablo and Briones Reservoirs and the residential communities of Lafayette, Orinda and Moraga.

Western Region: The Berkeley Hills

The hills above Berkeley stand in sharp contrast to those of the Northern Region. Heavily wooded redwood forests thrive here, nurtured by the cool breezes and moisture-laden fogs, which typically come in from the west. The hills are higher and steeper and reward those cyclists who like the challenge of elevation gain and the exhilaration of the long descents. A wide variety of off-road cycling is available in the Berkeley Hills, by virtue of four outstanding Regional Parks located in the region: Redwood, Anthony Chabot, Tilden and Wildcat Canyon.

Central Region: Mount Diablo

Mount Diablo serves as a focal point for the East Bay. Easily the highest peak, at an elevation of 3849 feet, the mountain dominates the landscape and can be seen from nearly everywhere in the Bay Area. The towns of Walnut Creek, Alamo, Danville and Clayton surround the mountain and serve as access points to the roads leading into the marvelous Mount Diablo State Park. Located on the eastern slope of Mount Diablo lies one of the most remote roads in the East Bay — Morgan Territory Road.

Southern Region: Fremont and Livermore

The Livermore Valley is home to some of the finest vineyards in northern California and has the added distinction of being the location of the unique power generating windmill farms in the windy Altamont Pass. Cycling through this area is certainly one of the most unusual and eerie experiences imaginable, especially when the wind is blowing and the blades are turning. Old and new are dramatically represented in the Southern Region by the historic Mission San José in Fremont and the ultra modern Lawrence Livermore National Laboratory in Livermore, while nearby, rural country roads, such as Palomares Road, near Sunol, and Calaveras Road, near Fremont, are surprisingly easy to find.

SAN FRANCISCO EAST BAY AREA

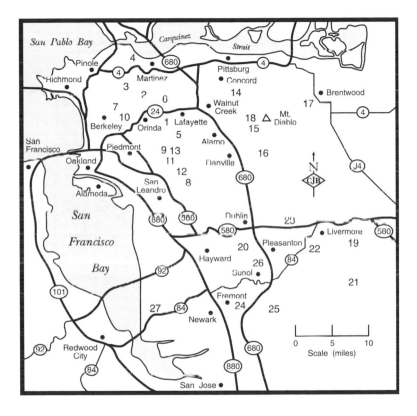

HOW TO USE THIS BOOK

Ride Parameters

At the beginning of each ride description is a short list of ride parameters. These are intended to give you a quick summary of that particular ride and to permit you to sort through the rides to find the one that best suits your needs.

Ride Rating — Reflects the overall difficulty of the ride, a simple judgement and classification into one of three possible categories: *Easy, Moderate* or *Difficult.* This usually depends upon the distance and the total elevation gain of the ride, and is affected by the steepness of the grades.

Total Distance — Indicates the length of the ride, excluding any optional side trips, which may be described in the ride.

Riding Time — Gives an indication of how much time to budget for the ride. Keep in mind, however, that this does not include extended stops for sightseeing, eating and resting. The riding time usually assumes an average pace of about 8-10 miles per hour.

Total Elevation Gain — Combines the elevation gains of all the climbing required. For example, climbing two hills, each with 500 feet of elevation gain, would result in 1000 feet of total elevation gain.

Calories Burned — Estimates the total amount of energy burned. This is based upon an average calorie burn rate of about 300 calories/hour on a flat road at about 14 miles/hour and about 800 calories/hour on a hill climb with about 8% grade with a speed of about 4 miles/hour. Some variations will occur for individual differences or for external factors.

Type of Bike — Suggests the use of a road or mountain bike. Although a ride may have a stretch of dirt road, it may still be suitable for a road bike, providing it is smooth and safe. Elaboration on this issue is usually found in the section on terrain.

Terrain

The road conditions, expected car traffic and general terrain are briefly described to permit you to quickly determine if the ride is right for you.

Ride Description

This section contains a general description of the ride, along with any interesting background or historical information for the area. Points of interest along the way are also highlighted. The general route to be followed is explained, although the details are saved for the *Ride*

Details and Mile Markers section. Extra side trip options, if applicable, are also outlined.

Starting Point

The exact place to start the ride is described, along with detailed directions explaining how to get there. In general, rides are started at locations where free parking is readily available and where refreshments can be purchased for either before or after your ride and are typically easily recognizable places with public restrooms available, making it easy for groups of people meeting to ride together.

Elevation Profiles

An elevation profile for each ride provides a detailed graph of the required hill climbs. These not only preview the terrain for you, but can be a useful reference to take with you on your ride, since they can help prepare you for the hills to be encountered along the way. Grades, in percent, for significant hill climbs are often indicated on the diagrams. A 10% grade is one that has about 500 vertical feet of elevation gain for each mile of distance.

Maps

Each ride has a map associated with it indicating the route. Rides with more than one option are indicated with direction arrows for each. In general, however, the map is not necessary for following the route, since detailed directions are included in the *Ride Details and Mile Markers* section. For clarity, the starting point of each ride is indicated on the map by an asterisk enclosed by a circle. ✪

Ride Details and Mile Markers

Directions for the route are described, along with the elapsed distance for each item. You don't need a cycle computer for this, since the markers come at frequent intervals and you will quickly learn to estimate distances accurately enough. The markers indicate the required turns to take in order to follow the route, as well as point out special sights and features of the ride that you might otherwise miss.

Ride Options

Some rides include two different variations. These are generally indicated with a suffix designation, A or B, to distinguish them. In most cases, the variations are offered to give the rider different levels of difficulty from which to choose. A separate *Ride Details and Mile Markers* section for each variation ensures that there is no confusion about the ride directions and essentially results in each variation being treated as a separate ride.

Northern Region

The Carquinez Strait and Lafayette

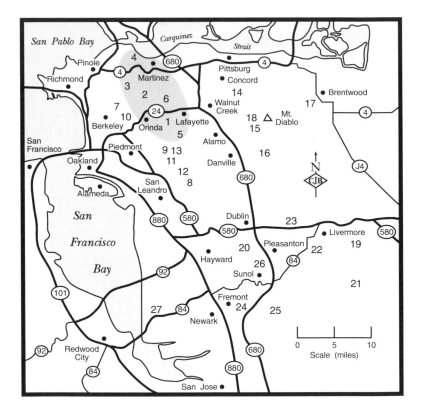

1 LAFAYETTE
Lafayette — Orinda — Briones Loop

	Ride 1A	Ride 1B
Region:	Northern	
Ride Rating:	Moderate	Difficult
Total Distance:	21 miles	33 miles
Riding Time:	2 hours	3 hours
Total Elevation Gain:	1500 feet	1900 feet
Calories Burned:	750	1000
Type of Bike:	Road Bike	Road Bike

Ride Description

The pleasant residential towns of Lafayette, Moraga and Orinda, and the rural countryside along Bear Creek Road, highlight this pair of rides, much favored by local cyclists and racing clubs. The presence of Briones Reservoir and Briones Regional Park, both on Bear Creek Road, ensure the encroachment of developers will be minimized into the distant future. Both rides require substantial hill climbing, although the grades are not terribly steep and no one climb is very long.

Starting Point

Start either ride in central Lafayette, at the intersection of Mount Diablo Boulevard and Moraga Road. To get there, take Highway 24 and get off at the Pleasant Hill Road exit for Central Lafayette. Take Pleasant Hill Road south one block and turn right onto Mount Diablo Boulevard. Proceed for about one mile to the Moraga Road intersection and park anywhere nearby.

Ride 1A (Moderate)

The ride leads out of Lafayette to Moraga on Moraga Road and then to Orinda on Moraga Way. Past Orinda, the countryside begins on Bear Creek Road as it travels past Briones Reservoir. The return to Lafayette is through the Happy Valley residential area along Happy Valley Road.

Terrain

The first half of the ride follows roads which carry moderate amounts of car traffic over mildly rolling hills. There are substantial climbs in the second half of the ride on Bear Creek Road and on Happy Valley Road.

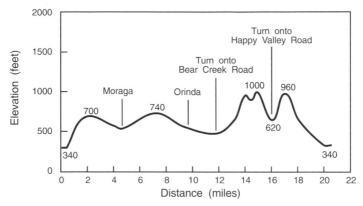

Ride 1A: Ride Details and Mile Markers

0.0   Proceed SOUTH on Moraga Road, heading toward Moraga.

1.9   Crest of hill — 700 feet.

4.7   Turn RIGHT onto Moraga Way.

9.3   Town of Orinda to the right — bear left to stay on main road which becomes Camino Pablo.

9.6   Highway 24 underpass.

11.8   Turn RIGHT onto Bear Creek Road.

15.0   Crest of hill — 1000 feet.

16.0   Turn RIGHT onto Happy Valley Road.

17.1   Crest — 960 feet.

18.2   Continue STRAIGHT at intersection with Upper Happy Valley Road.

20.1   Highway 24 underpass.

20.2   Turn LEFT onto Mount Diablo Boulevard.

20.6   Back at the start point.

Ride 1B (Difficult)

The route starts by following Moraga Road, leading to the town of Moraga, and Moraga Way, to Orinda. Past Orinda, the route follows rural roads as it leads past Briones Reservoir and Briones Regional Park along Bear Creek Road. Alhambra Valley Road, Reliez Valley Road and Pleasant Hill Road provide the return to Lafayette.

Terrain

The majority of the ride is along lightly traveled country roads, although substantial car traffic will usually be encountered along the roads to Moraga and Orinda. Most of the roads have bike lanes or an adequate shoulder, but there are some stretches where this is not the

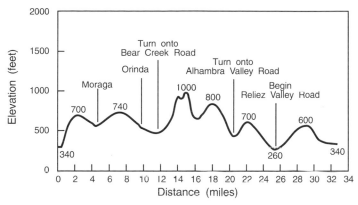

case. Although nearly 2000 vertical feet of climbing are required, it is spread out over six different hills.

Ride 1B· Ride Details and Mile Markers

0.0   Proceed SOUTH on Moraga Road, heading toward Moraga.

1.9   Crest of hill — 700 feet.

4.7   Turn RIGHT onto Moraga Way.

9.3   Town of Orinda to the right — bear left to stay on main road which becomes Camino Pablo.

9.6   Highway 24 underpass.

11.8   Turn RIGHT onto Bear Creek Road.

15.0   Crest of hill — 1000 feet.

16.0   Happy Valley Road intersection on the right side.

16.3   Briones Regional Park on right side.

20.3   Turn RIGHT onto Alhambra Valley Road.

21.8   Crest of hill — 700 feet.

25.2   Continue STRAIGHT to get on Reliez Valley Road.

29.4   Crest of hill — 600 feet.

30.6   Turn RIGHT onto Pleasant Hill Road.

31.5   Highway 24 underpass.

31.6   Turn RIGHT onto Mount Diablo Boulevard.

32.9   Back at the start point.

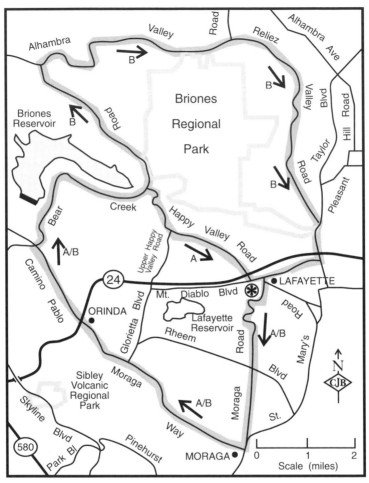

Ride Nos. 1A and 1B

San Pablo Reservoir >

2 ORINDA
San Pablo — Briones Reservoir Loop

Region: *Northern*
Total Distance: *24 miles*
Total Elevation Gain: *1300 feet*
Type of Bike: *Road Bike*

Ride Rating: *Moderate*
Riding Time: *2-3 hours*
Calories Burned: *800*

Terrain

The majority of the ride is on wide country roads with adequate shoulders and very little car traffic. Two substantial hill climbs are encountered in the latter part of the ride along Bear Creek Road.

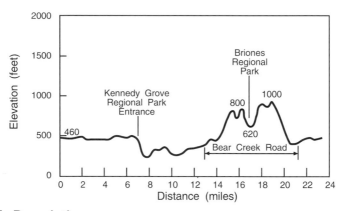

Ride Description

The San Pablo and Briones Reservoirs, both part of the East Bay watershed, are the focal points for this very popular cycling route. The landscape is generally wide open, with few trees but many broad vistas. Grassy oak-lined slopes, deep blue colors of the reservoirs, and usually blue skies combine to make this ride one of the most beautiful and pristine in the East Bay.

After leaving Orinda, the route along Camino Pablo and San Pablo Dam Road passes by San Pablo Reservoir and leads to Castro Ranch Road and then to Alhambra Valley Road with its many ranches. Bear Creek Road skirts Briones Regional Park and Briones Reservoir and completes the loop back to Camino Pablo. Along Bear Creek Road, there are two significant hill climbs, affectionately known as "Mama Bear" and "Papa Bear," respectively, which will challenge you with their 7% grades.

Starting Point

Start the ride in central Orinda at the corner of Camino Pablo and Brookwood Road. To get there, take Highway 24 to the Orinda exit at Camino Pablo. Proceed south about 1 block on Camino Pablo and park anywhere near the Brookwood Road intersection.

Ride Details and Mile Markers

0.0 Proceed NORTH on Camino Pablo, crossing under the freeway.

2.3 Continue STRAIGHT at the intersection with Wildcat Canyon Road on the left and Bear Creek Road on the right. Road becomes San Pablo Dam Road.

7.1 Kennedy Grove Regional Park on the right.

7.7 Turn RIGHT onto Castro Ranch Road.

10.0 Turn RIGHT onto Alhambra Valley Road.

12.8 Turn RIGHT onto Bear Creek Road.

16.2 "Mama Bear" crest — 800 feet.

17.8 Briones Regional Park on the left side.

18.1 Happy Valley Road intersection on the left side.

19.1 "Papa Bear" crest — 1000 feet.

21.2 Turn LEFT onto Camino Pablo, heading back toward Orinda.

23.2 Highway 24 underpass.

23.5 Back at Orinda.

Briones Reservoir, as seen from Bear Creek Road

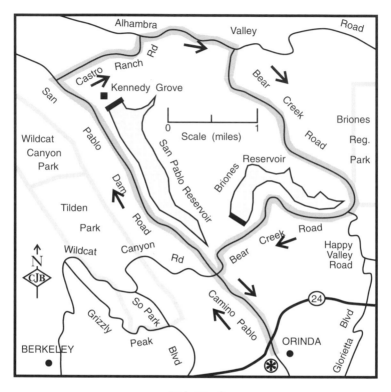

Ride No. 2

3   PINOLE
Pinole — Martinez Loop

Region: *Northern*
Total Distance: *30 miles*
Total Elevation Gain: *1300 feet*
Type of Bike: *Road Bike*

Ride Rating: *Moderate*
Riding Time: *3 hours*
Calories Burned: *900*

Terrain

The roads are mostly country roads with little traffic. Two exceptions are one stretch in Martinez and another near the end of the ride through Rodeo, both of which have substantial traffic along fairly busy city streets. There is one significant hill climb required, "Pig Farm Hill," along Alhambra Valley Road. The rest of the route is either flat or has only modest hills.

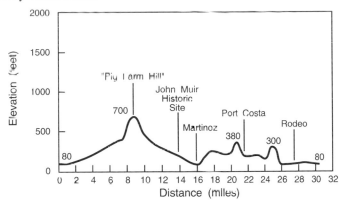

Ride Description

Pinole Valley Road and Alhambra Valley Road lead out of Pinole and into the quiet countryside of the Alhambra Valley with its many orchards and ranches. In Martinez is the John Muir National Historic Site, former home of the famed naturalist and founder of the Sierra Club. Open to the public with a nominal visitor fee, the home is completely furnished in the style of the era and is a worthwhile stopping point. Also on the property is the Vicente Martinez adobe, an old and historic building which was the home of one of the earliest settlers in the region.

After passing through central Martinez, the route leads along the beautiful Carquinez Scenic Drive, a twisting road with spectacular views of the Carquinez Strait. Although the road is washed out and closed to car traffic in one section, cyclists can still safely use it, although extra caution is advised at all times. Along Carquinez Scenic Drive, the tiny town of Port Costa makes for an interesting side trip. A former busy shipping port, it has a small harbor and some shops and restaurants.

The towns of Crockett and Rodeo are homes to numerous sugar and oil refineries, the most notable being the massive C&H Sugar Refinery in Crockett. A key element in the community, C&H Sugar is notable not only for its value as an employer, but also for its many financial contributions for the construction of municipal buildings and parks.

Starting Point

Start the ride in central Pinole, at the intersection of San Pablo Avenue and Tennent Avenue. To get there, take Highway 80 and get off at the Pinole Valley Road exit. Follow Pinole Valley Road north, where it becomes Tennent Avenue, and continue to San Pablo Avenue, about 1/2-mile from the freeway exit.

Ride Details and Mile Markers

0.0 Proceed SOUTH on Tennent Avenue, heading inland.

0.4 Begin Pinole Valley Road.

0.7 Highway 80 underpass.

3.5 Begin Alhambra Valley Road.

4.1 Intersection with Castro Ranch Road on the right.

6.9 Intersection with Bear Creek Road on the right.

8.4 "Pig Farm Hill" crest — 700 feet.

12.2 Turn LEFT to stay on Alhambra Valley Road. Reliez Valley Road continues to the right.

13.1 Turn LEFT onto Alhambra Avenue.

13.7 Highway 4 underpass.

13.8 John Muir National Historic Site on the left.

15.7 Turn LEFT onto Escobar Street in central Martinez.

15.9 Turn RIGHT onto Talbart Street.

16.1 Begin Carquinez Scenic Drive.

16.3 Carquinez Strait Regional Shoreline on left side.

18.1 Gate — begin washed out section of road.

19.8 Gate — return to maintained road.

20.6 Crest — 380 feet.

21.0 Reservoir Road on the right side — take this road for side trip to Port Costa.

22.1 Carquinez Strait Regional Shoreline on right side.

23.2 Begin Pomona Street in Crockett.

24.2 Highway 80 underpass.

25.1 Crest — 300 feet.

27.4   Town of Rodeo — begin Parker Avenue.

29.1   Bear RIGHT onto San Pablo Avenue.

30.4   Back at the start point in central Pinole.

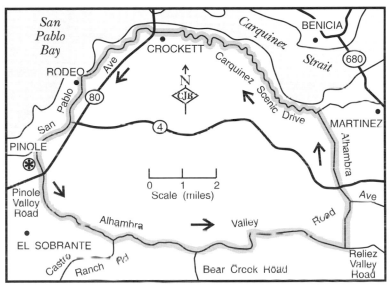

Ride No. 3

4 PORT COSTA
Port Costa Loop

Region: Northern	**Ride Rating:** Moderate
Total Distance: 19 miles	**Riding Time:** 2 hours
Total Elevation Gain: 1300 feet	**Calories Burned:** 700
Type of Bike: Road Bike	

Terrain

The roads in this ride carry very little traffic, except for sections through Martinez and Crockett. There is one hill to climb along Franklin Canyon Road and Cummings Skyway, but the 2-3% grade is a fairly modest one. Carquinez Scenic Drive, early in the ride, has a damaged section closed to car traffic, but is passable for bicycles.

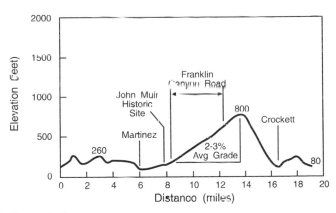

Ride Description

In the 1870s, Port Costa was a busy port, receiving large quantities of wheat and grain from Central Valley suppliers for the markets of the Bay Area. Although the resident population was only about 300, large numbers of sailors and dockworkers filled the town and provided the impetus for the operation of numerous saloons and hotels. Later, as the railroads became the main transportation for these supplies, the port became quiet. Today, the flavor of those bygone days is still present in Port Costa, with the old wheat warehouse converted to house quaint shops and restaurants and the Burlington Hotel still standing near the waterfront.

The route of this ride leaves Port Costa along the aptly named Carquinez Scenic Drive, from where the strait with its busy cargo shipping can be viewed. In Martinez, you will pass by the John Muir National Historic Site, former home of the famed naturalist. Maintained by the National Park Service, the property also holds the Vicente Martinez adobe, a fine example of early California architecture and lifestyle.

Franklin Canyon Road climbs steadily past oaks, orchards and corrals to Cummings Skyway. After one last uphill section, Cummings Skyway takes you on a rapid descent into Crockett for the return along Carquinez Scenic Drive back to Port Costa.

Starting Point

Start the ride in the small town of Port Costa, in the parking lot at the end of Canyon Lake Road on the waterfront. To get there from Concord and points east, take the McEwen Road exit from Highway 4 and follow McEwen Road north to its end at Carquinez Scenic Drive. Cross over onto Reservoir Street and turn right on Canyon Lake Road into Port Costa. From Richmond and the west, there is no exit for McEwen Road, so you must get off Highway 4 at Cummings Skyway and follow Franklin Canyon Road to get to McEwen Road.

Ride Details and Mile Markers

0.0   Take Canyon Lake Road through town, away from the waterfront.

0.2   Turn LEFT onto Reservoir Road.

0.7   Turn LEFT onto Carquinez Scenic Drive.

1.0   Crest — 260 feet.

1.8   Gate — begin damaged road section.

3.5   Gate — return to maintained road.

5.3   Carquinez Strait Shoreline Regional Park on the right side.

5.6   Begin Talbart Street, which turns left and becomes Escobar Street, heading into Martinez.

5.8   Turn RIGHT onto Berrellesa Street.

6.5   Merge into Alhambra Avenue.

7.7   John Muir National Historic Site on the right side.

7.8   Highway 4 underpass, then turn RIGHT onto Franklin Canyon Road, just past the railroad underpass.

11.5   McEwen Road intersection on the right side.

12.2   Turn RIGHT onto Cummings Skyway.

13.7   Crest — 800 feet.

14.4   Bear RIGHT onto Crockett Boulevard, heading toward Crockett.

16.4   Turn RIGHT onto Pomona Street in central Crockett.

17.0   Begin Carquinez Scenic Drive.

18.1   Carquinez Strait Shoreline Regional Park on the left side.

18.7   Turn LEFT onto Canyon Lake Road, heading into Port Costa.

19.2   Back at the start point.

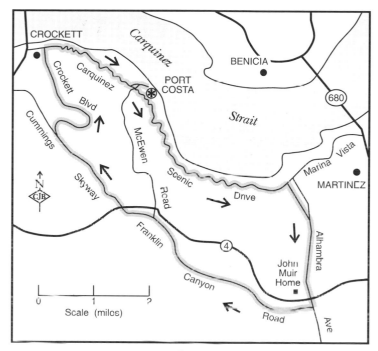

Ride No. 4

Carquinez Strait, as seen from Carquinez Scenic Drive

5　LAFAYETTE
Lafayette-Moraga Regional Trail

Region: *Northern*　　　　　　**Ride Rating:** *Easy*
Total Distance: *15 miles*　　　**Riding Time:** *1-2 hours*
Total Elevation Gain: *600 feet*　**Calories Burned:** *400*
Type of Bike: *Road Bike*

Terrain

The Lafayette-Moraga Regional Trail is a paved pathway for use by cyclists, equestrians, hikers and runners. Cyclists must yield to others at all times. There is one short section of the route on surface streets in Moraga, but bike lanes are present for safety. One slight hill must be traversed in each direction along the trail, but the grade is quite mild.

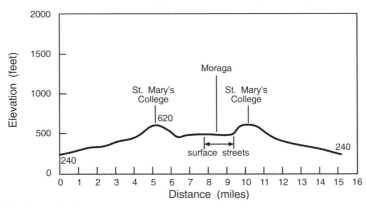

Ride Description

Administered by the East Bay Regional Park District and stretching from Lafayette to Moraga, this trail leads through residential neighborhoods but surprisingly retains the natural feel of a much more remote area. From the staging area on Pleasant Hill Road, the trail passes through Lafayette and then roughly follows parallel to St. Mary's Road. After crossing St. Mary's Road, a gradual climb leads to the crest of the hill at the St. Mary's College campus, visible off to the left. Just past the college at Moraga Road is a busy park and playground, Moraga Commons, at which public restrooms and water are available. The trail ends at Canyon Road at the Valle Vista Staging Area for EBMUD (East Bay Municipal Utilities District). Canyon Road leads back to Moraga Commons for the return back to Lafayette along the trail.

Starting Point

Start the ride in Lafayette, at the intersection of Pleasant Hill Road and Olympic Boulevard. To get there, take the Pleasant Hill Road exit from Highway 24 in Lafayette and follow Pleasant Hill Road south for about ½-mile to the Olympic Boulevard intersection. Park anywhere nearby and begin the ride at the trailhead on Pleasant Hill Road.

Ride Details and Mile Markers

0.0 Proceed WEST on Lafayette-Moraga Regional Trail, accessible from Pleasant Hill Road.

1.6 Short section on Brookdale Court, then continue on trail.

2.8 Cross wooden bridge.

3.2 Cross St. Mary's Road and continue trail on far side of the road.

4.8 Cross Rheem Boulevard.

5.0 St. Mary's College on the left side.

5.9 Moraga Commons — cross Moraga Road and continue trail on far side.

6.1 Trail ends - continue along School Street.

6.5 Cross Country Club Drive and turn RIGHT on sidewalk to get to trail

6.6 Turn LEFT to get back on trail.

6.8 Cross wooden bridge.

7.8 End of the trail — turn LEFT onto Canyon Road. Valle Vista Staging Area for EBMUD is on the far side of the road.

8.9 Cross Moraga Way and begin Moraga Road.

9.3 Cross St. Mary's Road and turn RIGHT onto trail into the Moraga Commons Park just across the intersection.

10.2 St. Mary's College on the right side.

10.4 Cross Rheem Boulevard.

12.1 Cross St. Mary's Road.

12.4 Cross wooden bridge.

13.6 Brookdale Court section.

15.0 Continue through Olympic Boulevard Staging Area parking lot to stay on trail.

15.2 Back at the start point at Pleasant Hill Road.

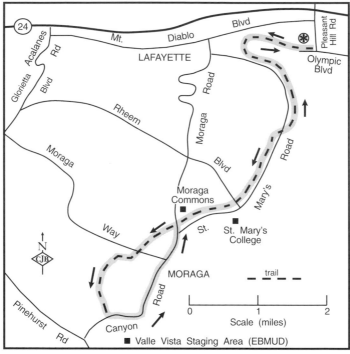

Ride No. 5

Lafayette-Moraga Regional Trail

6 LAFAYETTE
Mountain Bike Tour of Briones Regional Park

Region: *Northern*
Total Distance: *10 miles*
Total Elevation Gain: *1700 feet*
Type of Bike: *Mountain Bike*

Ride Rating: *Difficult*
Riding Time: *2-3 hours*
Calories Burned: *1000*

Terrain

The route follows wide fire trails across hills that are quite steep in places. Trails are well-marked and detailed maps are usually available at the park entrance.

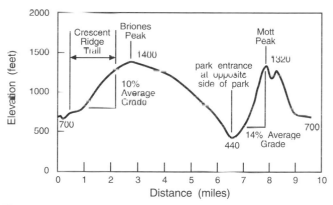

Ride Description

In the early 1800s, the land in what is today Briones Regional Park was settled by Felipe Briones. After passing through the hands of successive owners, the property was eventually acquired as part of the larger East Bay watershed and, later still, transferred to the East Bay Regional Park District for use as recreational open space for residents. Today, the 5,303 acres serve the needs of equestrians, hikers and cyclists.

This ride consists of a general tour of Briones Park, following the crests high above and around the park whenever possible. Stunning views of the distant countryside in all directions add to the grandeur of this energetic ride. Grass and oak covered slopes, heavily forested canyons, and an occasional meadow give the cyclist a general flavor of the park and add to the temptation to further explore the many other trails in a later visit.

After passing through a small meadow, the route climbs very steeply along Crescent Ridge Trail. Views from Briones Crest Trail and Briones Peak (elevation 1400 feet) are followed by a gradual descent to the far entrance of the park. After a short stretch on a paved section of Briones Road, Pine Tree Trail leads to Toyon Canyon Trail and another steep climb to Mott Peak. The steep descent on Black Oak Trail leads to another meadow and the return along Old Briones Road to the parking area.

Starting Point

Start the ride at the parking lot at the Bear Creek Road entrance to Briones Regional Park. To get there, take the Pleasant Hill Road exit off Highway 24 in Lafayette. Go south on Pleasant Hill Road and immediately turn right onto Mt. Diablo Boulevard. Follow Mt. Diablo Boulevard for about 1.5 miles and turn right onto Happy Valley Road. At the end of Happy Valley Road, about 4 miles distant, turn right onto Bear Creek Road and look for the entrance to Briones Regional Park on the right side. There is a nominal fee for parking within the park.

Ride Details and Mile Markers

0.0 Proceed out of the parking area into Briones Park on Old Briones Road Trail.

0.1 Continue past the gate and then turn RIGHT onto Homestead Valley Trail.

0.4 Continue past the gate, through the meadow and then turn LEFT onto Crescent Ridge Trail.

0.9 Archery Range on right side, then begin steep climb.

1.7 Bear RIGHT to stay on Crescent Ridge Trail (Yerba Buena Trail intersection on left).

2.2 Continue past gate, then turn LEFT onto Briones Crest Trail.

2.7 Bear LEFT to stay on Briones Crest Trail (Table Top Trail intersection on the right).

2.8 High point — 1400 feet.

4.2 Turn RIGHT onto Old Briones Road Trail.

4.7 Bear LEFT to stay on Old Briones Road Trail (Spengler Trail intersection on right).

5.4 Continue past gate onto paved road.

5.8 Turn LEFT onto Pine Tree Trail at the gate on left side of road.

6.2 Turn LEFT onto Toyon Canyon Trail.

6.5 Low point — 440 feet.

7.0 Bear LEFT onto Lagoon Trail.

7.6 Turn RIGHT onto Mott Peak Trail.

7.8 Bear LEFT to stay on Mott Peak Trail.

7.9 Crest — 1320 feet.

8.1   Turn LEFT onto Black Oak Trail.

8.3   Crest — 1300 feet.

8.9   Turn RIGHT onto Old Briones Road Trail.

9.4   Continue past gate.

9.5   Paved road begins.

9.6   Back at the start point.

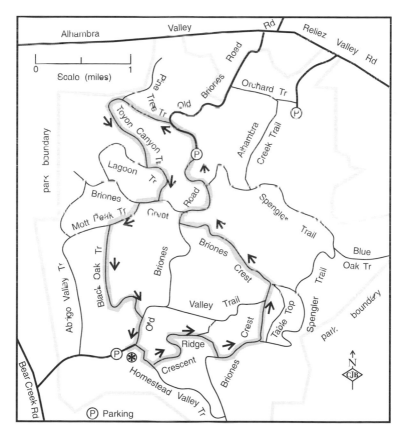

Ride No. 6

Western Region
The Berkeley Hills

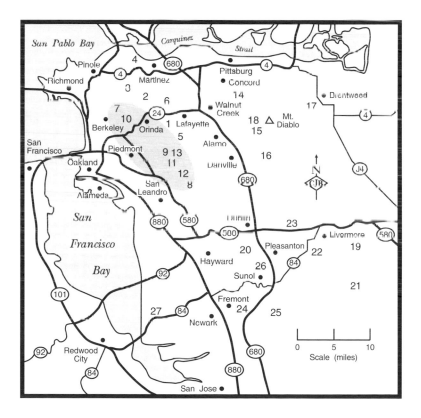

7 BERKELEY
Berkeley and the Oakland Hills

	Ride 7A	Ride 7B
Region:	*Western*	
Ride Rating:	*Difficult*	*Difficult*
Total Distance:	*27 miles*	*34 miles*
Riding Time:	*3 hours*	*3-4 hours*
Total Elevation Gain:	*2600 feet*	*3600 feet*
Calories Burned:	*1200*	*1600*
Type of Bike:	*Road Bike*	*Road Bike*

Ride Description

The lush and heavily forested Berkeley Hills contrast sharply with the grassy oak-covered hills around Lafayette and make this set of rides one of the most interesting in the East Bay. Energetic students from U.C. Berkeley mingle with established career people on weekends to make the roads along these routes some of the most popular among avid local cyclists. Hill climbs in both directions will provide plenty of challenge for even the most aggressive riders.

Starting Point

Start the ride in Berkeley, at the intersection of Ashby Avenue and Claremont Avenue. To get there, take Highway 13 and follow the signs to Berkeley. Highway 13 becomes Ashby Avenue. Parking can be found along Claremont Avenue, east of the Ashby Avenue intersection, in one of the many turnouts along the side of the road.

Ride 7A (Difficult)

The route for Ride 7A leads through beautiful Tilden Park, home to steam trains, the botanic gardens, golf course, merry-go-round, and numerous secluded trails and natural sights. Once past Tilden Park, at Inspiration Point lookout, the road descends into the Moraga Valley on the east side of the Berkeley Hills. A right turn onto Camino Pablo then leads through the residential town of Orinda and continues on to Moraga along Moraga Way. At Moraga, the return route follows along remote, wooded Canyon Road, and then climbs on Pinehurst Road and Skyline Boulevard past the Robert Sibley Volcanic Regional Preserve before descending along Tunnel Road back to the start point.

Terrain

Although the ride is only 27 miles long, it starts out with a rather steep (9%) climb into the Berkeley Hills and requires another climb later to get back. The roads are generally free of heavy car traffic, but bike lanes and wide shoulders are scarce, so caution is advised.

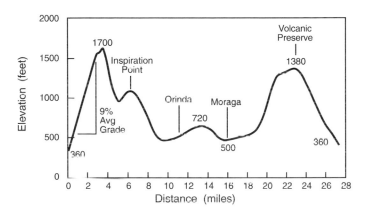

Ride 7A: Ride Details and Mile Markers

0.0 Proceed EAST on Claremont Avenue.

2.2 Turn LEFT onto Grizzly Peak Boulevard.

3.2 Lomas Cantadas Road on the right (Tilden Park steam trains).

3.5 Turn RIGHT onto South Park Drive, heading down into Tilden Park.

5.0 Turn RIGHT onto Wildcat Canyon Road.

6.3 Inspiration Point lookout on the left side.

8.9 Turn RIGHT onto Camino Pablo toward Orinda.

11.1 Highway 24 underpass.

11.4 Town of Orinda on the left side — begin Moraga Way.

16.0 Turn RIGHT onto Canyon Road.

17.2 Turn RIGHT onto Pinehurst Road.

21.2 Continue STRAIGHT at intersection to get on Skyline Boulevard.

22.3 Huckleberry Botanical Regional Preserve on the right side.

22.8 Robert Sibley Volcanic Regional Preserve on the right side.

24.3 Begin Old Tunnel Road.

26.0 Turn LEFT and then RIGHT to get on Tunnel Road.

26.4 Continue STRAIGHT at intersection to stay on Tunnel Road.

27.2 Back at the start point.

Ride 7B (Difficult)

Like Ride 7A, the route for Ride 7B leads through Tilden Park to Inspiration Point lookout and descends into the Moraga Valley to Camino Pablo. Instead of taking the right turn onto Camino Pablo, however, Ride 7B continues straight along Bear Creek Road past San Pablo and Briones Reservoirs, mainstays of the East Bay watershed. Happy Valley Road leads to Lafayette by passing through the peaceful residential area of Happy Valley. In Lafayette there are many fine restaurants and delicatessens to relax at before returning to Berkeley.

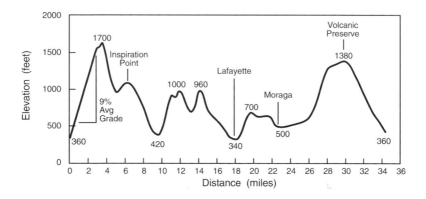

From Lafayette to Moraga along Moraga Road, there can be substantial traffic, but once past Moraga, Canyon Road becomes less busy and more beautiful as it passes through heavily wooded sections leading to Pinehurst Road and then Skyline Boulevard. Tunnel Road provides the return into Berkeley along a long and winding descent.

Terrain

Like Ride 7A, this ride also crosses the Berkeley Hills twice. In addition, there are several other substantial climbs required around Lafayette. The town of Lafayette is at about the halfway point and makes a nice resting spot to break up the trip.

Ride 7B: Ride Details and Mile Markers

0.0 Proceed EAST on Claremont Avenue.

2.2 Turn LEFT onto Grizzly Peak Boulevard.

3.2 Lomas Cantadas Road on the right side (Tilden Park steam trains).

3.5 Turn RIGHT onto South Park Drive, heading down into Tilden Park.

5.0 Turn RIGHT onto Wildcat Canyon Road.

6.3 Inspiration Point lookout on the left side.

8.9 Continue STRAIGHT at intersection with Camino Pablo Road and begin Bear Creek Road.

12.0 Crest of hill — 1000 feet.

13.0 Turn RIGHT onto Happy Valley Road toward Lafayette.

14.1 Crest of hill — 960 feet.

15.2 Continue STRAIGHT at intersection with Upper Happy Valley Road.

17.1 Highway 24 underpass.

17.2 Turn LEFT onto Mount Diablo Boulevard into central Lafayette.

17.6 Turn RIGHT onto Moraga Road.

19.5 Crest of hill — 700 feet.

23.0 Begin Canyon Road.

24.2 Turn RIGHT onto Pinehurst Road.

28.2 Continue STRAIGHT at intersection to get on Skyline Boulevard.

29.3 Huckleberry Botanical Regional Preserve on the right side.

29.8 Robert Sibley Volcanic Regional Preserve on the right side.

31.3 Begin Old Tunnel Road.

33.0 Turn LEFT and then RIGHT to get on Tunnel Road.

33.4 Continue STRAIGHT at intersection to stay on Tunnel Road.

34.2 Back at the start point.

Bear Creek Road

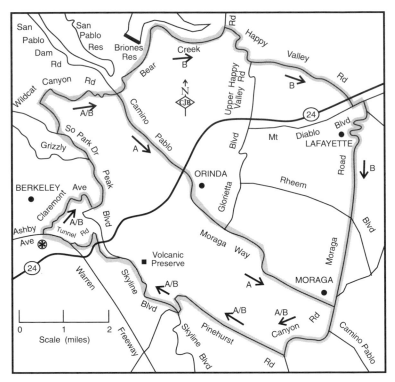

Ride Nos. 7A and 7B

8 SAN LEANDRO
Around Lake Chabot Regional Park

Region: *Western*
Total Distance: *25 miles*
Total Elevation Gain: *1700 feet*
Type of Bike: *Road Bike*

Ride Rating: *Moderate*
Riding Time: *2-3 hours*
Calories Burned: *900*

Terrain

The roads are mostly free of heavy traffic, except for the short section along MacArthur Boulevard and Foothill Boulevard in San Leandro, where it can be fairly hectic and where extra caution is advised. Two extended climbs are encountered, the first, of about 1000 feet in elevation gain and the second, about 400.

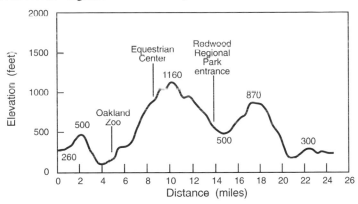

Ride Description

Lake Chabot, part of the East Bay Municipal Utilities District (EBMUD) water supply for the City of Oakland, is located within Anthony Chabot Regional Park. Encompassing nearly 5000 acres, the park is home to many other recreational activities, such as camping, picnicking, horseback riding, hiking and mountain biking. This ride follows a route completely around the park along mostly rural roads, with the exception of the section in San Leandro.

Starting at the entrance to the Lake Chabot Marina, the route leads along the hills overlooking the lake and then down into San Leandro. After a short stretch along busy city streets, a long sustained climb along Golf Links Drive, Grass Valley Road and Skyline Boulevard takes you to the high point, 1160 feet above sea level, and to some spectacular views of the East Bay cities below.

Redwood Road then descends past the entrance to Redwood Regional Park to a low point near the intersection with Pinehurst Road. A relatively short climb along lightly traveled Redwood Road, with views of Upper San Leandro Reservoir on the left, is followed by a long exhilarating descent to Seven Hills Road for the return to the marina starting point.

Starting Point

Start the ride at the entrance for the Lake Chabot Marina on Lake Chabot Road, just east of San Leandro. To get there, take Highway 580 to San Leandro and get off at the exit for Fairmont Drive. Follow Fairmont Drive east up the hill, turn left onto Lake Chabot Road and park anywhere near the turnoff for Lake Chabot Marina.

Ride Details and Mile Markers

0.0   Proceed NORTH on Lake Chabot Road, heading toward San Leandro.

0.2   Turn RIGHT to stay on Lake Chabot Road (Fairmont Drive is straight ahead).

2.5   Begin Estudillo Avenue.

2.8   Highway 580 underpass, then turn RIGHT onto MacArthur Boulevard.

3.4   Turn RIGHT onto Foothill Boulevard. You will have to cross several lanes of merging traffic to do this.

4.0   Continue STRAIGHT at 106th Avenue and turn RIGHT onto Stanley Avenue.

4.6   Turn RIGHT onto 98th Avenue.

4.7   Turn RIGHT onto Golf Links Road and cross under Highway 580. Knowland Park and the Oakland Zoo on the right side.

6.6   Continue STRAIGHT to get on Grass Valley Road (Golf Links Road turns to the right).

7.0   Turn LEFT onto Skyline Boulevard (Grass Valley Road ends at this point).

8.4   Chabot Equestrian Center on the right side.

10.2 High point — 1160 feet.

11.7 Turn RIGHT onto Redwood Road.

13.5 McDonald Staging Area for Chabot Park on the right side.

13.9 Redwood Regional Park entrance on the left side.

14.1 Pinehurst Road intersection on the left side.

16.0 Big Trees/Bort Meadow parking area for Chabot Regional Park on the right side.

17.4 Crest — 870 feet.

18.2 Marciel Gate for Chabot Regional Park on right side.

21.9 Golf course clubhouse on the right side.
23.0 Turn RIGHT onto Seven Hills Drive.
24.1 Turn RIGHT onto Lake Chabot Road.
24.6 Back at the start point.

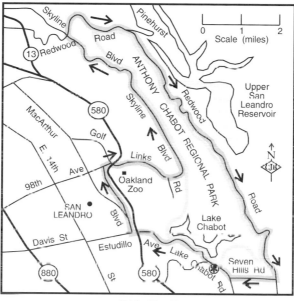

Ride No. 8

Upper San Leandro Reservoir, as seen from Redwood Road

9 PIEDMONT
Around Redwood Regional Park

Region: *Western*
Total Distance: *13.5 miles*
Total Elevation Gain: *1300 feet*
Type of Bike: *Road Bike*

Ride Rating: *Moderate*
Riding Time: *1-2 hours*
Calories Burned: *600*

Terrain

The roads are smooth and somewhat rural, but can carry substantial car traffic, especially on weekends. There is some climbing required in the beginning of the ride and again in the latter part.

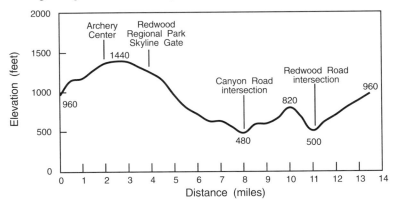

Ride Description

Redwood Regional Park, one of the many parks in the East Bay preserved for recreational uses, was once the proud home of majestic virgin redwoods. Extensive logging in the area, required for the construction of the homes of the East Bay cities, has long since stopped and the remaining redwoods have been allowed to flourish.

This ride follows a relatively short loop completely encircling the park. In the beginning climb of about 500 feet in elevation gain along Skyline Boulevard, spectacular views of the cities and San Francisco Bay to the west are revealed. Along Skyline Boulevard are several entrances for Redwood Regional Park, leading to hiking trails which you may want to explore before continuing your ride. Skyline Gate is especially good for this, since outstanding views of the park can be reached after only a short walk along the trails.

Just after Skyline Gate, the route follows Pinehurst Road on the far side of the park. From Pinehurst Road, after the Canyon Road intersection, views of Upper San Leandro Reservoir can be seen as you slowly climb and then descend. The return along Redwood Road is another challenging climb that will lead you back to the starting point at Skyline Boulevard.

Starting Point

Start the ride in the hills east of Piedmont at the corner of Redwood Road and Skyline Boulevard. To get there, take Highway 13 (the Warren Freeway) and get off at the exit for Redwood Road. Follow Redwood Road east up into the hills to its intersection with Skyline Boulevard. There is a shopping center with plenty of parking on the northeast corner of this intersection.

Ride Details and Mile Markers

0.0 Proceed NORTH on Skyline Boulevard.

0.6 Turn RIGHT to stay on Skyline Boulevard. (Joaquin Miller Road is straight ahead.)

1.6 Roberts Regional Recreation Area on the right side.

2.0 Redwood Archery Center on the right side.

3.0 Crest — 1440 feet.

3.8 Skyline Gate for Redwood Regional Park on the right side.

4.2 Turn RIGHT onto Pinehurst Road. (Shepherd Canyon Road is on the left.)

8.2 Continue STRAIGHT at the intersection with Canyon Road to stay on Pinehurst Road.

9.7 Crest — 820 feet.

11.0 Turn RIGHT onto Redwood Road.

13.4 Back at the start point.

View in Redwood Regional Park, near Skyline Gate

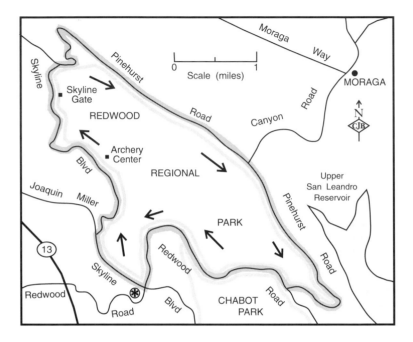

Ride No. 9

10 BERKELEY

Tilden and Wildcat Canyon Mountain Bike Ride

Region: *Western*
Total Distance: *17 miles*
Total Elevation Gain: *1700 feet*
Type of Bike: *Mountain Bike*

Ride Rating: *Moderate*
Riding Time: *2 hours*
Calories Burned: *1200*

Terrain

The trails in Tilden and Wildcat Canyon Regional Parks are wide fire roads and are steep and somewhat rough in some sections. A 4-mile stretch of the ride along Nimitz Way is paved and flat, however, and may be used by even the most casual riders. To do this section only, refer to the *Ride Details and Mile Markers* and pick up the ride at the 3.9 mile point.

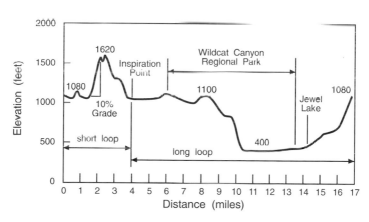

Ride Description

Tilden and Wildcat Canyon Regional Parks, located adjacent to each other in the hills to the east of Berkeley, are administered by the East Bay Regional Park District. Together, they encompass over 4,000 acres of forests with trails for cycling, hiking and equestrian use. In addition, Tilden Park includes a golf course, Botanic Garden, Steam Trains, pony rides, merry-go-round, Nature Area and Lake Anza. Weekends find the parks fully utilized, as the residents of the surrounding population centers come here to relax and to enjoy the natural beauty.

The first part of the ride consists of a short 4-mile loop through the southern section of Tilden Park. This section includes a fairly steep 500-foot climb and less ambitious riders may want to avoid it and to begin the ride at the start of the long loop at the 3.9-mile mark.

The long loop leads through the northern section of Tilden Park and includes a tour of Wildcat Canyon, as well. The first 4 miles follow a paved section of trail on Chester Nimitz Way, named for the famed World War II admiral. From this relatively flat section, there are stunning views of the surrounding areas visible in both directions. At the end of the paved trail, the route follows fire roads continuing along the crest of the hills and then down a steep descent into Wildcat Canyon. After riding through the canyon in the lower elevations, the route leads past serene Jewel Lake and then follows a forested trail as it climbs back to Inspiration Point.

Starting Point

Start the ride at Inspiration Point on Wildcat Canyon Road. To get there from the east, take Highway 24 to the Orinda exit and proceed north on Camino Pablo. Turn left onto Wildcat Canyon Road and follow it about 2.5 miles to Inspiration Point, on the right side.

From the west, take Ashby Avenue, in Berkeley, east to Claremont Avenue. Follow Claremont Avenue east up into the Berkeley Hills and turn left onto Grizzly Peak Boulevard. Turn right onto South Park Drive and right again onto Wildcat Canyon Road. After about 1.5 miles on Wildcat Canyon Road, Inspiration Point will be on the left side.

Ride Details and Mile Markers

0.0   Proceed out of the parking lot and turn RIGHT onto Wildcat Canyon Road.

0.2   Trailhead for Seaview Trail on the left.

0.4   Turn LEFT into Quarry Picnic Area and follow signs for the trail. Just past the picnic tables, get on Quarry Trail.

0.7   Bear RIGHT to stay on Quarry Trail.

1.5   Continue STRAIGHT to get on Big Springs Trail and proceed past the parking lot to continue on the trail at the far side. Begin climbing toward the ridge.

2.0   Turn LEFT onto Seaview Trail along the ridge.

2.4   Crest — 1620 feet.

3.3   Big Springs Trail intersection on the left side.

3.7   Turn RIGHT onto Wildcat Canyon Road at the end of the trail.

3.9   End of the short loop back at Inspiration Point. Begin the long loop by proceeding into Tilden Park through the gate onto the paved Nimitz Way, located just outside of the parking lot.

5.2   Laurel Canyon Trail intersection on the left side.

5.7 Wildcat Peak trail on the left side.

5.8 Enter Wildcat Canyon Park at cattleguard. San Pablo Reservoir visible below on the right side.

6.1 Conlon Trail intersection on the left side.

8.0 Veer LEFT onto gravel trail and continue past gate.

8.2 Turn LEFT onto Mezue Trail and then RIGHT onto San Pablo Ridge Trail. Steep descent begins.

9.4 Bear LEFT onto Belgum Trail.

9.5 Clark Boas Trail intersection on right side.

10.3 Continue STRAIGHT at the gate and then turn LEFT onto the old paved road toward Tilden Nature Area. This road leads to Wildcat Creek Trail.

11.1 Turn RIGHT off road and continue on paved section to gravel trail just ahead (Wildcat Creek Trail).

12.1 Mezue Trail intersection on left behind gate.

12.3 Rifle Range Road Trail intersection on right side.

13.5 Enter Tilden Nature Area.

14.3 Jewel Lake on right side. Bear LEFT just past lake onto Loop Trail.

14.8 Bear RIGHT to stay on Loop Trail.

15.1 Turn LEFT to stay on Loop Trail and continue past gate onto paved road.

15.3 Turn LEFT at the Lone Oak Picnic Ground to get on fire trail and then bear RIGHT onto Wildcat Gorge Trail.

16.1 Turn LEFT onto Curran Trail.

16.6 Bear RIGHT at Meadow Canyon Trail intersection on the left.

16.8 Back at Inspiration Point.

San Pablo Reservoir, as seen from Nimitz Way

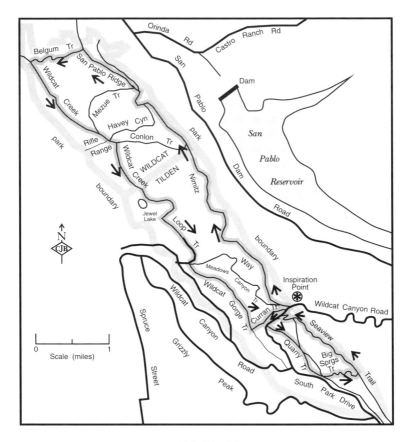

Ride No. 10

East Bay Bike Trails

11 PIEDMONT
Short Loop Around and Through Chabot Regional Park

Region: *Western*
Total Distance: *11 miles*
Total Elevation Gain: *900 feet*
Type of Bike: *Mountain Bike*

Ride Rating: *Easy*
Riding Time: *1 hour*
Calories Burned: *400*

Terrain

This short ride follows smooth roads, which carry some traffic, and includes a 2.5-mile stretch on dirt trails to cut through Chabot Regional Park. Although rated as a mountain bike ride, the route can easily be followed on a road bike, provided the tires are rugged enough to sustain some bumps and loose stones.

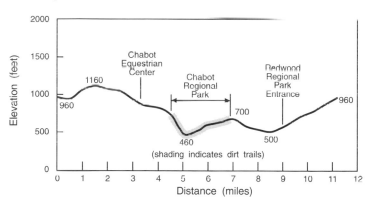

Ride Description

The route initially follows Skyline Boulevard as it climbs for a short distance, offering some stunning views of the cities of the East Bay to the west. After passing the high point at 1160 feet above sea level, the road descends on a slight downhill grade as it skirts Chabot Regional Park. Just 50 yards or so before Skyline Boulevard ends and Grass Valley Road continues to the right, there is a gate marking an entrance into Chabot Regional Park on the left side.

Once inside the gate, an unpaved fire road leads downhill along Jackson Grade. After crossing a small stone bridge and making a left turn onto Grass Valley Trail, you climb a gentle slope as the route leads through the center of the park, a small valley in which you will often see livestock grazing. At the end of Grass Valley Trail is a paved service road, which leads up a small hill and out of the park. A left turn onto Redwood Road is followed by a descent to the intersection with Pinehurst Road and then along a challenging climb for the last 4 miles back to the starting point.

Starting Point

Start the ride in the hills east of Piedmont at the corner of Redwood Road and Skyline Boulevard. To get there, take Highway 13, the Warren Freeway, and get off at the exit for Redwood Road. Follow Redwood Road east up into the hills to its intersection with Skyline Boulevard. There is a shopping center with plenty of parking on the northeast corner of this intersection.

Ride Details and Mile Markers

0.0   Proceed SOUTH on Skyline Boulevard.

2.4   Hansom Avenue intersection on right side.

3.3   Chabot Equestrian Center on left side.

4.5   Turn LEFT onto a fire road just before Skyline Boulevard ends and Grass Valley Road begins. The fire road is just beyond a gate into Chabot Regional Park. Once on the trail, continue STRAIGHT onto Jackson Grade (Lake Chabot Bike Loop).

5.0   Bear RIGHT onto Brandon trail, cross a small stone bridge, and then turn LEFT onto Grass Valley Trail.

5.1   Livestock gate.

5.5   Redtail Trail intersection on the right side.

5.8   Livestock gate.

6.5   Livestock gate and then turn RIGHT onto a paved service road up the hill.

6.8   Turn LEFT at the end of the road onto Redwood Road.

8.7   Intersection with Pinehurst Road on the right.

9.0   Redwood Regional Park entrance on the right side.

9.5   McDonald Staging Area for Chabot Park on the left side.

11.3   Back at the start point.

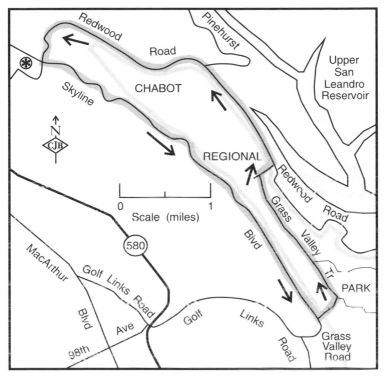

Ride No. 11

Grass Valley Trail

12 SAN LEANDRO
Anthony Chabot Regional Park Mountain Bike Ride

Region: *Western*
Total Distance: *20 miles*
Total Elevation Gain: *2200 feet*
Type of Bike: *Mountain Bike*

Ride Rating: *Difficult*
Riding Time: *3-4 hours*
Calories Burned: *1000*

Terrain

Three separate hill climbs give this ride plenty of challenge, even for aggressive riders. With the exception of an extended paved section along Lake Chabot, the route follows unpaved fire roads with loose rocks and plenty of bumps.

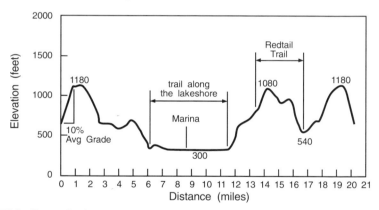

Ride Description

Anthony Chabot Regional Park, located east of San Leandro, encompasses almost 5000 acres of land and Lake Chabot. The lake, part of the watershed serving the water supply needs of Oakland and other East Bay cities, is also used extensively for recreational purposes. Boating, fishing, camping and picnicking are just a few of the many activities possible on and around the lake.

This mountain bike ride covers 20 miles of trails and completely traverses the park. The route begins at one of the rear accesses into the park, at the MacDonald Staging Area along Redwood Road, and immediately climbs on a steep grade along MacDonald Trail. Expansive views at the crest are brief, as the trail drops sharply into the valley below. Passing through Grass Valley along the Brandon Trail, you will often encounter grazing cattle at close range. After a short climb at the end of the valley, the trail then descends and follows a paved path, leading around Lake Chabot. More people will usually be present around the lake, since this area of the park has more activities and attracts families with children on weekends.

After more than 5 miles along the edge of the lake, the route crosses a narrow wooden bridge, where you will need to walk your bike, and then continues along the far side of the lake, where the dirt trails resume. A steep climb of about 800 feet in elevation gain takes you away from the lake and back into the more remote sections of the park, as it passes through some camping areas along the crest of the mountains. After riding along the ridge for a short section, a steep descent back into Grass Valley is followed by a climb back up MacDonald Trail and the final descent back to the starting point.

Starting Point

Start the ride at the MacDonald Staging Area for Chabot Regional Park on Redwood Road. To get there, take Highway 13, the Warren Freeway, and get off at the exit for Redwood Road. Follow Redwood Road east up into the hills and continue past the intersection with Skyline Boulevard for about 2 miles to the MacDonald Staging Area on the right side.

Ride Details and Mile Markers

0.0   Proceed out of the parking area into Chabot Park on the MacDonald Trail leading out of the left side of the parking area.

1.1   Turn LEFT to stay on MacDonald Trail (Park Ridge Gate to the right side).

1.7   Continue past livestock gate.

2.5   Continue past livestock gate, then turn RIGHT toward Bort Meadow and Grass Valley.

2.6   Turn LEFT onto wide trail at the bottom of the hill.

2.7   Turn RIGHT toward Brandon Trail, then turn LEFT onto Brandon Trail.

4.1   Turn RIGHT to get on Jackson Grade (Lake Chabot Bicycle Loop).

4.6   Skyline Boulevard gate on the right side. Do not go through gate, but continue ahead on the trail, now called Goldenrod Trail.

5.5   Begin paved section for short distance.

5.6   Turn LEFT off paved section onto continuation of Goldenrod Trail.

6.0   Continue STRAIGHT on Bass Cove Trail, toward Marina.

7.0   Continue STRAIGHT across paved service road and begin West Shore Trail.

7.1	Cross dam.
8.7	Marina on the left side. Just past the Marina, turn LEFT in picnic area, cross wooden bridge, then turn LEFT onto trail continuing along the lake. This is East Shore Trail.
10.4	Continue past gate and begin dirt trail.
10.6	Turn LEFT to cross narrow wooden bridge, then turn LEFT onto Honker Bay Trail along lake shore.
11.7	Begin climbing.
12.4	Continue STRAIGHT on paved road through campground.
13.0	Continue past the park entrance booth and get on the Towhee Trail, parallel to the right side of the road.
13.4	Turn LEFT onto Brandon Trail.
13.6	Turn RIGHT onto Redtail Trail, just before the road.
14.0	Cross road and continue on Redtail Trail.
14.8	Bear RIGHT to stay on Redtail Trail and cross road.
15.1	Turn RIGHT onto road and then turn LEFT to get on continuation of Redtail Trail on far side of the road.
15.7	Begin steep descent.
16.7	Turn RIGHT onto Grass Valley Trail.
17.6	Continue past gate toward Bort Meadow and then turn RIGHT onto small trail up the hill toward MacDonald Trail.
17.7	Turn LEFT onto MacDonald Trail to return to the MacDonald Staging Area.
19.4	Begin descent.
20.3	Back at the start point.

Redtail Trail

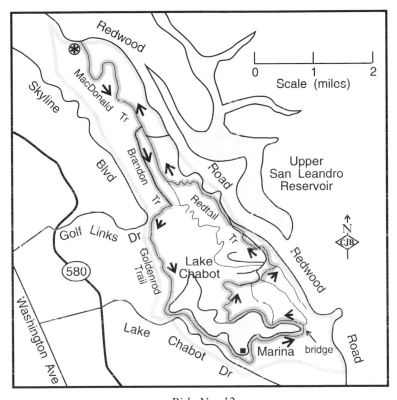

Ride No. 12

13 SAN LEANDRO
Redwood Regional Park Mountain Bike Ride

Region: *Western*
Total Distance: *10 miles*
Total Elevation Gain: *1200 feet*
Type of Bike: *Mountain Bike*

Ride Rating: *Moderate*
Riding Time: *2 hours*
Calories Burned: *500*

Terrain

The route generally follows wide unpaved fire trails with loose stones. Some very steep sections in the beginning will require all but the strongest riders to walk their bikes.

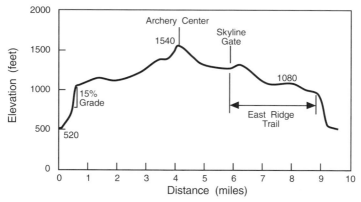

Ride Description

Redwood Regional Park is today home to giant redwood trees descended from original growth trees logged for construction. The park consists of a central valley surrounded by mountains and is rich with trails for hiking, biking and equestrian use. As is the case with all parks administered by the East Bay Regional Park District, bikes are restricted to fire roads and must yield at all times to both hikers and equestrians.

This route follows around the park periphery along the mountain ridges, affording spectacular views in all directions. Beginning at a trailhead near the park headquarters, the route immediately climbs on a very steep grade on the West Ridge Trail. Expect to walk your bike up the steep sections and console yourself as you do this with the fact that once up onto the ridge, the remainder of the ride will have only modest climbing.

From the west ridge, the equestrian center can be seen below. Continuing past the Roberts Recreation Area and the Archery Range at the high point of the ride, 1540 feet above sea level, the first scenes of the valley, in the central part of the park, can be seen. After Skyline Gate, the East Ridge Trail allows you to cruise on a gentle downhill grade to the intersection for Canyon Trail, which takes you on a steep descent to the valley floor and the paved service road leading back to the starting point.

Starting Point

Start the ride at the main entrance for Redwood Regional Park on Redwood Road. To get there, take Highway 13, the Warren Freeway, and get off at the exit for Redwood Road. Follow Redwood Road east up into the hills and continue past the intersection with Skyline Boulevard for about 2 miles to the entrance for Redwood Regional Park on the left side. Park anywhere and start the ride at the first trailhead on the left side of the road entering the park, at the Fern Hut/Mill Site, Fishway Interpretive Center.

Ride Details and Mile Markers

0.0   Proceed out of the parking area into Redwood Regional Park toward Middle Trail and turn RIGHT onto Middle Trail.

0.1   Turn LEFT onto West Ridge Trail.

0.4   Golden Spike Trail intersection on the left side.

0.5   Very steep section begins.

0.6   Toyon Trail intersection on the left side.

0.9   Orchard Trail intersection on the right, followed by Tate Trail intersection on the left.

1.2   Turn LEFT onto Baccharis Trail.

1.7   Turn LEFT onto Dunn Trail.

2.8   Bear RIGHT to get on Graham Trail.

3.4   Trail intersection for Roberts Park on the left side.

3.9   Turn LEFT to get back onto West Ridge Trail.

4.1   Archery Center on the right side.

4.2   Continue past the gate to stay on West Ridge Trail.

4.6   Moon Gate on the left side.

4.8   Tres Sendas Trail intersection on the right side.

5.3   French Trail intersection on the right side.

5.9   Skyline Gate Staging Area. Continue straight ahead and begin East Ridge Trail.

7.2   Prince Road on the right side.

8.9   Turn RIGHT onto Canyon Trail.

9.3   Turn LEFT onto the paved road at the end of the trail.

9.6   Back at the start point.

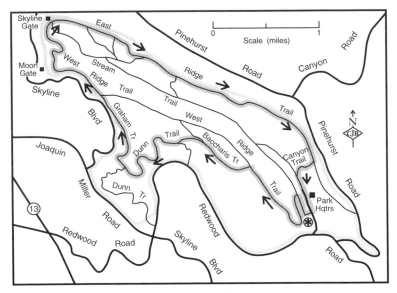

Ride No. 13

West Ridge Trail, near Skyline Gate

Central Region
Around Mount Diablo

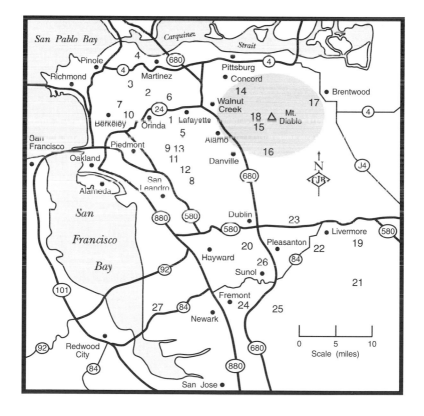

14 WALNUT CREEK
Contra Costa Canal Trail

Region: *Central*
Total Distance: *19 miles*
Total Elevation Gain: *150 feet*
Type of Bike: *Road Bike*

Ride Rating: *Easy*
Riding Time: *2 hours*
Calories Burned: *400*

Terrain

The route is very flat and follows a smooth, paved trail devoid of car traffic, with the exception of a 3.5-mile stretch along busy surface streets. The trail crosses over busy residential streets in many places and extra caution is advised. Cyclists share the trail with pedestrians and equestrians and must yield to both at all times.

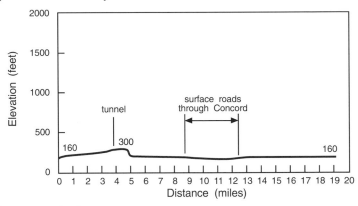

Ride Description

The Contra Costa Canal was constructed over many years and finally put into operation in the 1950s. Originally intended to serve as irrigation for local agriculture, the canal today is used as the water supply for many of the East Bay cities. It is owned and operated by the Contra Costa Water District, but through lease agreements with the East Bay Regional Park District, the multi-use Contra Costa Canal Trail was built.

Beginning at Heather Farms Park, this ride first follows Briones-Mt. Diablo Trail south along the canal and then loops back to the Contra Costa Canal Trail. The trail ends at Willow Pass Road, where surface streets through central Concord connect to the other end of the trail in Pleasant Hill along Chilpancingo Parkway for the return back to Heather Farms.

Starting Point

Start the ride in Walnut Creek at Heather Farms Park. To get there, get off Highway 680 in Walnut Creek at Ygnacio Valley Road and follow Ygnacio Valley Road east for about 2 miles to San Carlos Drive. Turn left onto San Carlos Drive and park your car near the park. Begin mileage at the corner of San Carlos Drive and Heather Drive.

Ride Details and Mile Markers

0.0 Proceed WEST on Heather Drive with the park on your right and the tennis courts on your left.

0.1 Turn LEFT onto Marchbanks Drive.

0.2 Turn RIGHT onto Ygnacio Valley Road.

0.3 Turn LEFT at the crosswalk for the John Muir Medical Center on the left side to get on the Briones-Mount Diablo Regional Trail on the far side of the road.

0.6 Continue STRAIGHT at the junction at which the Briones-Mount Diablo Regional Trail branches to the right.

2.1 Cross Walnut Avenue and continue on trail as it follows parallel to the road.

3.3 Golf course on the right side.

3.8 Bear RIGHT at the far end of the golf course to stay on the trail.

3.9 Walk your bike through dark tunnel which crosses under Ygnacio Valley Road.

4.7 Steep downhill section. Continue straight at trail intersection to begin Contra Costa Canal Trail.

5.3 Cross Treat Boulevard at the pedestrian crosswalk.

8.7 Turn LEFT onto Willow Pass Road at the end of bike path.

9.4 Turn RIGHT onto East Street in central Concord.

9.6 Turn LEFT onto Bonifacio Street.

10.0 Turn RIGHT onto Concord Avenue.

10.2 Freeway 242 underpass.

11.5 Freeway 680 underpass and begin Chilpancingo Parkway.

12.3 Turn LEFT onto Contra Costa Canal Trail at the top of the hill.

13.6 Cross over Taylor Boulevard by using the pedestrian crosswalk to the right.

13.8 Las Juntas Park on the left side.

17.4 Highway 680 underpass.

18.3 Turn RIGHT to cross the wooden bridge on the right side — an information board is on the left — and head toward Heather Farms Park.

18.4 Turn RIGHT onto the service road and then LEFT to get back on the bike path. Continue on the bike path as it winds around the right shore of the lake.

19.0   Continue through the parking lot and turn LEFT onto Heather Drive.

19.1   Back at the start point.

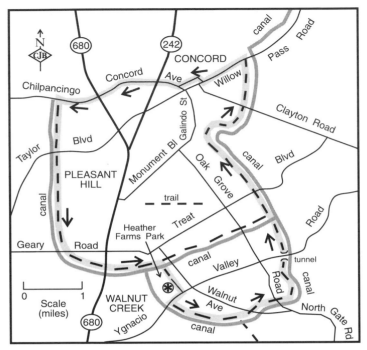

Ride No. 14

Contra Costa Canal and Trail

15　ALAMO
Mount Diablo Road Rides

	Ride 15A	Ride 15B
Region:	Central	
Ride Rating:	Difficult	Difficult
Total Distance:	28 miles	52 miles
Riding Time:	2-3 hours	4-5 Hours
Total Elevation Gain:	2100 feet	2700 feet
Calories Burned:	1100	1600
Type of Bike:	Road Bike	Road Bike

Ride Description

Mount Diablo dominates the landscape of the East Bay as its summit towers to an elevation of 3849 feet above sea level. The roads on each side of the mountain are a cyclists delight, carrying little car traffic and exposing backcountry scenery, which belies their proximity to the dense population centers nearby. The hill climbs are challenging and the remoteness is extraordinary.

Starting Point

Start the rides in Alamo at the Alamo Plaza shopping center on Danville Boulevard, just north of the intersection with Stone Valley Road. To get there, take Highway 680 to Danville and get off at the Stone Valley Road exit. Proceed west on Stone Valley Road, turn right on Danville Boulevard and look for Alamo Plaza on the left side along Danville Boulevard.

Ride 15A (Difficult)

This route heads north into busy Walnut Creek along wide bike lanes on Danville Boulevard. Hectic surface streets in Walnut Creek are followed by the rural northern access into Mount Diablo State Park along stunningly scenic North Gate Road. The population centers below expand into view as you climb steadily through the oak-studded hillsides of the eastern slope. At the park headquarters and ranger station at the intersection with Summit Road and South Gate Road, riders with extra energy can challenge themselves with an optional climb to the mountain top about 4.5 miles away and 1800 feet higher on Summit Road.

From the park headquarters, South Gate Road leads downhill along a winding descent to leave the park and meet with Diablo Road. Diablo

Road, Green Valley Road and Stone Valley Road take you back to the starting point in Alamo.

Terrain

Expect substantial car traffic from Alamo and through Walnut Creek, but fewer cars in Mount Diablo State Park. There is a long, sustained climb of about 2000 feet in elevation gain into the park, followed by a long descent out the other end to Danville.

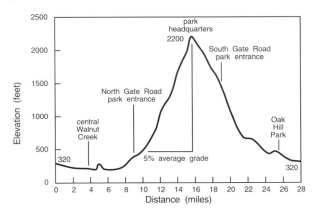

Ride 15A: Ride Details and Mile Markers

0.0   Proceed NORTH on Danville Boulevard.

2.0   Cross Rudgear Road and begin South Main Street.

2.6   Cross under Highway 680.

3.5   Cross Mount Diablo Boulevard in central Walnut Creek.

3.8   Turn RIGHT onto Civic Drive.

4.2   Turn RIGHT onto Ygnacio Valley Road.

4.4   Continue STRAIGHT across Walnut Boulevard.

5.9   Turn RIGHT onto Walnut Avenue.

7.5   Turn RIGHT onto Oak Grove Road and then LEFT onto North Gate Road.

8.9   Park entrance booth — no fee for bikes.

15.1   2000 foot elevation marker on right side.

15.5   Turn RIGHT onto South Gate Road (Summit Road continues straight ahead to the top of the mountain).

18.8   Park entrance booth on South Gate Road.

22.5   Turn RIGHT onto Diablo Road.

24.1   Turn RIGHT onto Green Valley Road.

24.8   Turn LEFT onto Stone Valley Road.

27.7   Cross under freeway and turn RIGHT onto Danville Boulevard.

28.0   Back at the start point.

Ride 15B (Difficult)

Ride 15B follows Danville Boulevard north to Walnut Creek and busy Ygnacio Valley Road east through Walnut Creek to Clayton, located due north of Mount Diablo. From Clayton, the route heads south along Clayton Road and then suddenly gets more peaceful along Marsh Creek Road. Some of the most remote country in the entire East Bay is experienced on Morgan Territory Road, as it climbs steadily along the eastern slope of Mount Diablo to an elevation of about 2000 feet. About 2 miles of road at this elevation is followed by a very steep and winding descent. Manning Road, Highland Road and Camino Tassajara take you past isolated ranches and country residences toward the impeccably manicured estates of Blackhawk. Blackhawk Road, Green Valley Road and Stone Valley Road complete this long and difficult loop.

Terrain

You will encounter significant car traffic from Alamo and through Walnut Creek and into Clayton before it thins out when you reach remote Morgan Territory Road on the eastern slope of Mount Diablo. Along Morgan Territory Road, there is a long and steady climb up to 2000 feet elevation and a steep descent down the other side. There are no services along Morgan Territory Road, so be sure to carry adequate supplies of water and snacks.

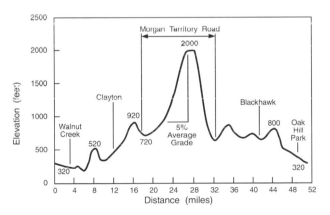

Ride 15B: Ride Details and Mile Markers

0.0   Proceed NORTH on Danville Boulevard.

2.0   Cross Rudgear Road and begin South Main Street.

2.6   Cross under Highway 680.

3.5   Cross Mount Diablo Boulevard in central Walnut Creek.

3.8   Turn RIGHT onto Civic Drive.

4.2   Turn RIGHT onto Ygnacio Valley Road.

6.9   Cross Oak Grove Road.

11.1 Turn RIGHT onto Clayton Road.

12.6 Turn RIGHT onto Marsh Creek Road.

16.6 Crest — 920 feet.

17.4 Turn RIGHT onto Morgan Territory Road.

26.8 Morgan Territory Regional Preserve on the left side.

28.3 Begin descent.

32.5 Turn RIGHT onto Manning Road.

33.3 Turn RIGHT onto Highland Road.

38.1 Turn RIGHT onto Camino Tassajara.

40.5 Blackhawk East Gate on the right side.

42.7 Turn RIGHT onto Blackhawk Road.

46.2 Mount Diablo Scenic Drive intersection on the right side.

47.8 Turn RIGHT onto Green Valley Road.

48.5 Turn LEFT onto Stone Valley Road.

51.4 Cross under freeway and turn RIGHT onto Danville Boulevard.

51.7 Back at the start point.

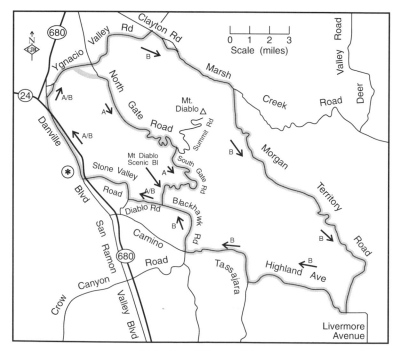

Ride Nos. 15A and 15B

Ranch entrance on North Gate Road >

16 DANVILLE
Blackhawk Loop

Region: *Central*
Total Distance: *11.5 miles*
Total Elevation Gain: *500 feet*
Type of Bike: *Road Bike*

Ride Rating: *Easy*
Riding Time: *1 hour*
Calories Burned: *300*

Terrain

This short, scenic ride follows residential roads that can have substantial car traffic. There are no steep climbs, but there is a steady 3% grade for about the first 4 miles.

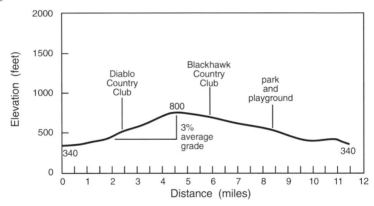

Ride Description

Beautiful ranches along Diablo Road, the lush country clubs at Diablo and Blackhawk, and the specter of mighty Mount Diablo rising in the east punctuate this easy ride in the East Bay. Starting in the town of Danville, site of the farm of one of the first settlers in the area, the route takes you east out of town along Diablo Road, heading directly toward Mount Diablo, the "Devil Mountain." As you ride along the tree-lined road past horse stables and ranches, look for the well-marked turn for Diablo Country Club. Take a short side-trip down this road and visit the grounds of this exclusive playground for well-heeled locals.

Past Diablo Country Club, the road changes name to become Blackhawk Road. Just over the crest of the hill, the exclusive Blackhawk residential area will appear on the left side, with the Blackhawk Country Club directly adjacent to the road. A right turn onto Camino Tassajara will lead past a park and playground on the right side and continue through residential areas to rejoin Diablo Road for the return to Danville.

Starting Point

Start the ride in Danville at the corner of Diablo Road and Hartz Avenue. To get there, take Highway 680 to Danville and get off at the exit for Diablo Road. Take Diablo Road west for about ½-mile to central Danville where there is plenty of parking.

Ride Details and Mile Markers

0.0 Proceed EAST on Diablo Road, heading away from Danville.

0.4 Highway 680 underpass.

0.7 Intersection with Camino Tassajara on right side.

1.8 Intersection with Green Valley Road on the left and McCauley Road on the right.

2.4 Diablo Country Club turn-off on the left side.

3.3 Begin Blackhawk Road at intersection with Mount Diablo Scenic Drive on the left.

4.6 Crest — 800 feet.

5.9 Blackhawk Country Club entrance on the left side.

6.9 Turn RIGHT onto Camino Tassajara.

8.3 Park and playground on the right side.

9.7 Turn RIGHT to stay on Camino Tassajara (Sycamore Valley Road is straight ahead).

10.9 Turn LEFT onto Diablo Road.

11.2 Highway 680 underpass.

11.5 Back at the start point.

Diablo Country Club in Danville

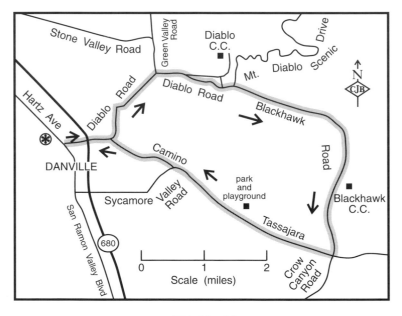

Ride No. 16

East Bay Bike Trails

17 **BRENTWOOD**
Brentwood Orchards Loop

Region: *Central*
Total Distance: *32 miles*
Total Elevation Gain: *600 feet*
Type of Bike: *Road Bike*

Ride Rating: *Moderate*
Riding Time: *3-4 hours*
Calories Burned: *800*

Terrain

This ride is quite flat except for two small hills at the midway point in the westernmost part of the route. Car traffic is generally minimal along most of the route, but you can expect heavy traffic with lots of trucks along Brentwood Boulevard, Lone Tree Way and Walnut Boulevard. Services are scarce, so take along adequate water and food.

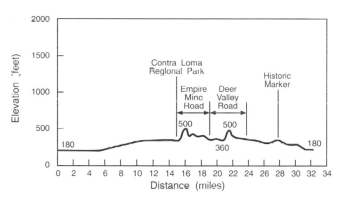

Ride Description

Located in the easternmost part of Contra Costa County, at the gateway to the expansive Delta to the east and in the shadow of majestic Mount Diablo to the west, Brentwood is alive with orchards and farms prospering on the rich soil of the area. In the spring, when the trees are in blossom, or in late summer, when the fruit is ripe, this ride is most pleasant.

Starting in the agricultural town of Brentwood, the route takes you east along quiet country roads through orchards and past farms to Byron Highway. Sunset Road, Eden Plains Road and Delta Road continue through the rural region and follow along the railroad tracks before the route heads west along Lone Tree Way, with its recently constructed residential housing developments.

Contra Loma Regional Park, in the westernmost part of the ride, is a good place to rest. Water and restrooms are available, as well as picnic areas and a swimming reservoir. Empire Mines Road and Deer Valley Road continue south with stunning views of Mount Diablo directly west. This section of the ride is hilly and may be windy, as well. Marsh Creek Road leads through a small canyon to Walnut Boulevard for the final stretch back to Brentwood.

Starting Point

Start the ride in central Brentwood, in the eastern part of the East Bay. To get there from the north, take Highway 4 east and then south all the way into Brentwood. From the south, take Highway 580 to the Vasco Road exit in Livermore and follow Vasco Road north to Brentwood, where it becomes Walnut Boulevard. Park anywhere near downtown and start the ride at the intersection of First Street and Oak Street.

Ride Details and Mile Markers

0.0   Proceed EAST on Oak Street.

0.2   Turn RIGHT onto Fourth Street.

0.3   Turn LEFT onto Chestnut Street.

3.0   Turn LEFT onto Byron Highway.

4.4   Turn LEFT onto Sunset Road as Byron Highway continues straight ahead.

5.4   Turn RIGHT onto Eden Plains Road.

6.5   Turn LEFT onto Delta Road.

8.2   Turn LEFT onto Brentwood Boulevard (Highway 4).

8.8   Turn RIGHT onto Lone Tree Way.

10.2   Cross railroad tracks.

12.2   Cross Hillcrest Avenue.

14.4   Turn LEFT onto Dallas Ranch Road.

14.6   Turn RIGHT onto Old Lone Tree Way.

15.2   Turn LEFT onto Empire Mine Road (Bluerock Drive is to the right). After you make this turn, the entrance to Contra Loma Regional Park will be on the right side. This is a good place to stop for a snack, if you have brought one with you. The park is about 1 mile down the access road.

15.9   Crest — 500 feet.

19.2   Turn RIGHT onto Deer Valley Road.

21.6   Crest — 500 feet.

22.4   Briones Valley Road intersection on the right.

23.6   Turn LEFT onto Marsh Creek Road.

26.9 Bear LEFT to stay on Marsh Creek Road. Camino Diablo continues to the right.

27.9 Reservoir and dam on the left side and historic marker on the right.

29.7 Turn LEFT onto Walnut Boulevard.

32.1 Turn RIGHT onto Oak Street.

32.3 Back at the start point.

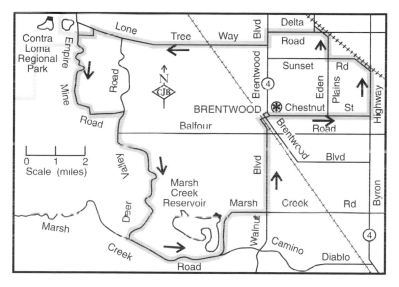

Ride No. 17

18 DANVILLE
Mount Diablo Mountain Bike Ride

Region: *Central*
Total Distance: *9 miles*
Total Elevation Gain: *1800 feet*
Type of Bike: *Mountain Bike*

Ride Rating: *Difficult*
Riding Time: *2 hours*
Calories Burned: *1100*

Terrain

This ride follows wide fire roads with some loose gravel. Trails are not always marked, so be careful to follow the route directions very carefully. Steep slopes, typical of off-road riding, should be anticipated. Poison oak is very common along the trails, so avoid contact with anything.

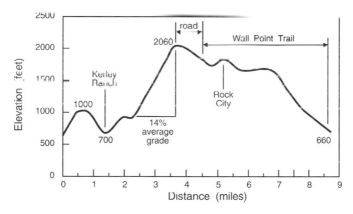

Ride Description

Dominating the landscape in the East Bay, Mount Diablo towers to a height of 3849 feet and can be seen from nearly anywhere in the Bay Area. Easily the largest single parkland in the East Bay, Mount Diablo State Park offers the visitor many miles of trails for hiking, cycling and horseback riding.

This ride is located in the western part of the park and is easily accessible from Alamo and Danville. It is ideal as an introduction to the park, by virtue of the wide variety of terrain and geology along the way and the stunning views of the distant summit above and the population centers below.

Starting at the historic Macedo Ranch Staging Area, the trail first leads uphill through active pastureland, where it is common to

< Railroad scene along Sunset Road

75

encounter grazing cattle up close. After this short climb, the route then leads down into Pine Canyon and follows along Pine Creek. The climb out of the canyon to Barbecue Terrace is a long and steep one, as the trail passes through grassy hillsides, and panoramic views begin to emerge. A short stretch along the main road leads to the trailhead for the return leg of the tour along Summit Trail and then Wall Point Road. Wall Point Road is a fire road that first leads through the large sandstone formations of Rock City and then along a narrow ridge with dramatic drop-offs in both directions. From the ridge, views of Danville and Walnut Creek are visible to the west and of the Mount Diablo Summit, to the east. Also to the east, you can look down into Pine Canyon and see where the earlier part of the ride took place. A long and sometimes steep descent takes you back to the starting point at Macedo Ranch.

Starting Point

Start the ride in Danville, at the end of Green Valley Road. To get there, take the Stone Valley Road exit from Highway 680 and follow Stone Valley Road east about three miles to Green Valley Road. Turn left onto Green Valley Road, follow it to the end, and park at the Macedo Ranch Staging Area.

Ride Details and Mile Markers

0.0 Proceed EAST on the Wall Point Road fire trail, located on the right side of the parking area.

0.3 Bear RIGHT to stay on Wall Point Road.

0.8 Turn LEFT onto Pine Canyon Trail. Wall Point Road is to the right.

1.3 Go past livestock gate and turn RIGHT onto Stage Road at Kerley Ranch.

1.5 Continue past livestock gate.

1.7 Continue STRAIGHT toward Barbecue Terrace. Buckeye Trail goes to the left.

2.3 Continue past livestock gate.

2.7 Single-track trail intersection on right side.

3.3 Continue past gate and turn RIGHT onto paved service road.

3.6 Turn RIGHT onto South Gate Road, the main road into the park.

4.5 Turn RIGHT onto Summit Trail toward Rock City. Trail head is in a small turnout on the right side of the road.

4.8 Trail ends back at the main road — turn RIGHT onto Wall Point Road fire road.

7.5 Bear RIGHT to stay on Wall Point Road. Emmons Canyon Road intersection on the left side.

7.9   Bear LEFT to stay on Wall Point Road toward Macedo Ranch. Pine Canyon Trail is on right side.

8.7   Back at the start point.

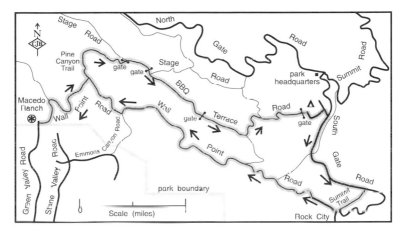

Ride No. 18

Barbecue Terrace Trail

Southern Region
Fremont and Livermore

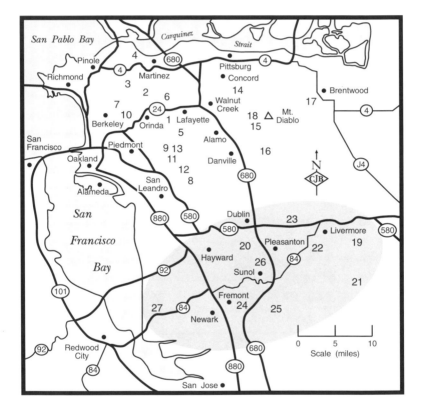

19 LIVERMORE

Riding through the Windmills of Livermore

	Ride 19A	Ride 19B
Region:	Southern	
Ride Rating:	Moderate	Difficult
Total Distance:	32 miles	44 miles
Riding Time:	3-4 hours	4-5 hours
Total Elevation Gain:	1700 feet	2500 feet
Calories Burned:	1000	1400
Type of Bike:	Road Bike	Road Bike

Ride Description

A common sight along Highway 580 as it climbs over Altamont Pass just east of Livermore is the vast array of windmills built to generate electrical power for northern California. Some little-used back-roads provide for a most unusual cycling experience on this pair of rides. Although the windmills are generally idle, windy days, especially common in the summer months, can find many of them operating. The noise of the whirring blades and the occasional crackling of static electricity create an eerie atmosphere in an otherwise very quiet place.

Starting Point

Start either of the rides in Livermore, at the intersection of First Street and South Livermore Avenue. To get there, take Highway 580 and get off at the Livermore Avenue exit. Proceed south on Livermore Avenue for about 1 mile to central Livermore, where there is plenty of parking along side streets.

Ride 19A (Moderate)

The route for Ride 19A leads east out of Livermore on South Livermore Avenue past the vineyards of Concannon and Wente Brothers. Cross Road then passes several ranches as it climbs steadily to meet with Patterson Pass Road. The long climb on Patterson Pass Road is usually made easier by a brisk tailwind. Once over the crest, the windmills come into view. Cruise by them slowly so you can get the full experience. The return along Altamont Pass Road has a much smaller climb, but it can seem quite difficult because the tailwinds on Patterson Pass Road become headwinds here. As you come back into the outskirts of town, you pass by the Lawrence Livermore National Laboratories, site of the largest nuclear weapons research and testing center in the country. An informative visitor center, open to the public and free of charge, explains the many facets of nuclear power.

Terrain

The roads around Livermore generally have only small amounts of car traffic, except for those within the city limits. There is a long climb on Patterson Pass Road and a smaller one on Altamont Pass Road. Winds are usually brisk and come in from the west.

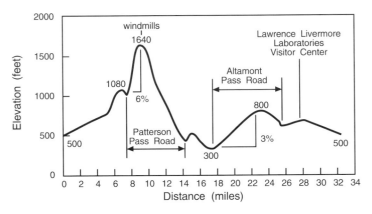

Ride 19A: Ride Details and Mile Markers

0.0   Proceed EAST on South Livermore Avenue (Highway J2).

2.4   Mines Road intersection on right side.

3.1   Vasco Road intersection on left side.

4.3   Greenville Road intersection on left side.

5.2   Turn LEFT on Cross Road.

6.9   Crest — 1080 feet.

7.4   Turn RIGHT on Patterson Pass Road.

9.2   Crest — 1640 feet.

13.0   Railroad underpass.

14.1   Turn LEFT onto Midway Road.

15.3   Crest — 520 feet.

16.2   Highway 580 underpass.

16.9   Turn LEFT onto Grant Line Road.

17.4   Bear RIGHT onto Altamont Pass Road.

21.6   Railroad underpass.

23.7   Carroll Road intersection on the left side.

25.1   Railroad trestle underpass.

25.4   Turn LEFT onto Greenville Road.

27.8 Lawrence Livermore National Laboratory Visitor Center on right side.

28.3 Turn RIGHT onto East Avenue.

32.0 Turn RIGHT onto South Livermore Avenue.

32.3 Back at the start point.

Ride 19B (Difficult)

Like Ride 19A, Ride 19B leads out of Livermore past the Concannon and Wente Brothers vineyards and tasting rooms and follows Cross Road and Patterson Pass Road through the windmills. Once past the windmills and down to the bottom on the other side of Patterson Pass, the route follows a gravel bike path along a 6-mile stretch of the California Aqueduct. The return to Livermore is along rural Corral Hollow Road and includes a very challenging climb across the 1640-foot summit, usually accompanied by brisk, annoying headwinds.

Terrain

Traffic is usually minimal, except for those sections inside Livermore city limits. Two difficult climbs are required, with the second harder than the first, by virtue of the prevailing westerly winds and the rather steep half mile section near the crest.

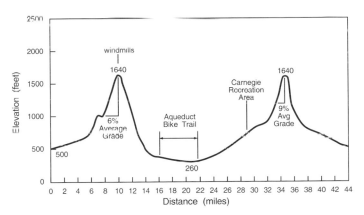

Ride 19B: Ride Details and Mile Markers

0.0 Proceed EAST on South Livermore Avenue (Highway J2).

2.4 Mines Road intersection on right side.

3.1 Vasco Road intersection on left side.

4.3 Greenville Road intersection on left side.

5.2 Turn LEFT on Cross Road.

6.9 Crest — 1080 feet.

7.4 Turn RIGHT on Patterson Pass Road.

9.2   Crest — 1640 feet.

13.0   Railroad underpass.

14.1   Midway Road intersection on the left side.

16.0   Cross Highway 580 overpass.

16.2   Turn RIGHT on Aqueduct Bike Trail just past aqueduct.

21.7   Turn RIGHT on Corral Hollow Road (road name is indicated on bridge spanning the aqueduct).

23.1   Cross Highway 580 overpass.

28.9   Carnegie Recreation Area on the left.

29.9   County line — begin Tesla Road.

33.6   Crest — 1640 feet.

38.6   Cross Road intersection on right side.

41.6   Mines Road intersection on left side.

43.9   Back at start point.

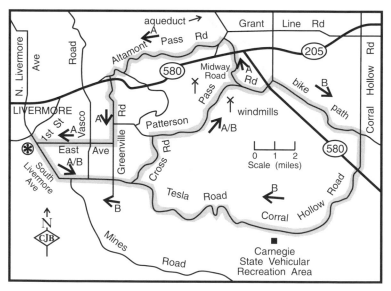

Ride Nos. 19A and 19B

Windmill farm in Patterson Pass >

20 DUBLIN
Palomares Road Ride

	Ride 20A	Ride 20B
Region:	*Southern*	
Ride Rating:	*Moderate*	*Difficult*
Total Distance:	*28 miles*	*38 miles*
Riding Time:	*2-3 hours*	*3-4 hours*
Total Elevation Gain:	*1500 feet*	*1900 feet*
Calories Burned:	*900*	*1200*
Type of Bike:	*Road Bike*	*Road Bike*

Ride Description

Pleasanton Ridge, rising to an elevation of about 1600 feet, is a dominant feature of the landscape just west of Highway 680 near Pleasanton. Roads, encircling the ridge, pass by golf courses, old railroad tracks, canyon streams, ranches and orchards and provide a favorite route for local cyclists. The old and the new are both represented, with one-room schoolhouses and dilapidated barns located within shouting distance of modern, glass-dominated office buildings.

Starting Point

Start the ride in Dublin, at the corner of Foothill Road and Stoneridge Drive. To get there take Highway 580 to the San Ramon Road exit and go south on Foothill Road to the intersection with Stoneridge Drive or take Highway 680 to the Stoneridge Drive exit and go west to the Foothill Road intersection.

Ride 20A (Moderate)

Ride 20A proceeds south along flat Foothill Road past contemporary residential neighborhoods and then into more rural areas as it leads to Sunol, a small one-street town, noted for its popularity with local motorcycle riders on weekends. A stretch on busy Niles Canyon Road is followed by a long and steady climb on Palomares Road into the quiet Stonybrook Canyon. Superb views from the crest of the hill are followed by a speedy descent into a valley with ranches lined with white fences. The return is along Dublin Canyon Road, following parallel to Highway 580 as it climbs through Dublin Canyon and then descends into Dublin.

Terrain

Substantial car traffic should be anticipated along busy Foothill Road and Niles Canyon Road. Keep to the right as much as possible along these sections. The two hill climbs, one along Palomares Road and the other along Dublin Canyon Road, will usually have very little traffic.

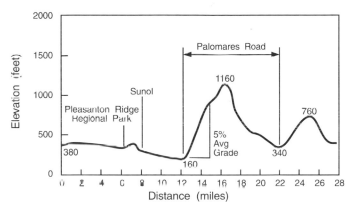

Ride 20A: Ride Details and Mile Markers

0.0 Proceed SOUTH on Foothill Road.

2.8 Intersection with Bernal Avenue on the left.

6.1 Pleasanton Ridge Regional Park on the right.

7.9 Turn LEFT on Kilkare Road and then RIGHT onto Main Street.

8.1 Merge RIGHT onto Niles Canyon Road.

12.0 Pass under railroad trestle and then turn RIGHT onto Palomares Road and begin climbing immediately.

16.7 Crest — 1160 feet.

21.9 Turn RIGHT onto Palo Verde Road.

22.3 Turn RIGHT onto Dublin Canyon Road.

25.0 Crest — 760 feet.

27.5 Turn RIGHT onto Foothill Road.

28.0 Back at the start point.

Ride 20B (Difficult)

The route for Ride 20B follows the same as Ride 20A until the final return leg to Dublin, along Dublin Canyon Road. Instead of turning onto Dublin Canyon Road, Ride 20B follows Castro Valley Boulevard to Crow Canyon Road. The ride north along Crow Canyon Road leads up a gentle grade and connects to Norris Canyon Road, on which a more substantial climb past remote ranches and pastureland is required. The return to Dublin along Bollinger Canyon Road and San Ramon

Boulevard is a gentle downhill usually accompanied by a friendly tailwind.

Terrain

Heavy traffic should be expected along many of the busy roads on this route. The climbs along Palomares Road and Norris Canyon Road will usually be free of traffic.

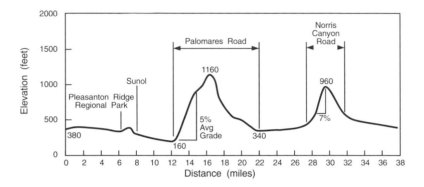

Ride 20B: Ride Details and Mile Markers

  0.0 Proceed SOUTH on Foothill Road.

  2.8 Intersection with Bernal Avenue on the left.

  6.1 Pleasanton Ridge Regional Park on the right.

  7.9 Turn LEFT on Kilkare Road and then RIGHT onto Main Street.

  8.1 Merge RIGHT onto Niles Canyon Road.

12.0 Pass under railroad trestle and then turn RIGHT onto Palomares Road and begin climbing immediately.

16.7 Crest — 1160 feet.

21.9 Turn LEFT onto Palo Verde Road.

22.2 Turn LEFT onto East Castro Valley Boulevard.

22.7 Highway 580 underpass.

24.0 Turn RIGHT onto Crow Canyon Road.

27.4 Turn RIGHT onto Norris Canyon Road.

29.6 Crest — 960 feet.

31.4 Turn RIGHT onto Bollinger Canyon Road.

32.3 Turn RIGHT onto San Ramon Valley Boulevard.

35.3 Alcosta Boulevard.

37.0 Highway 580 overpass.

37.8 Back at the start point.

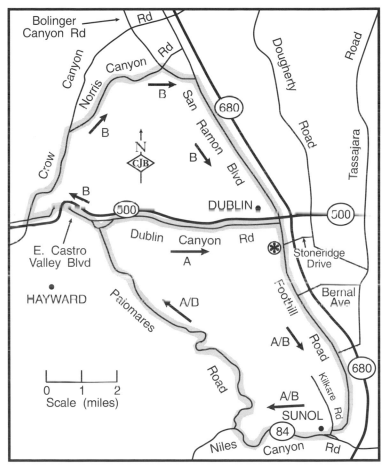

Ride Nos. 20A and 20B

21 LIVERMORE
Mines Road of Livermore

Region: *Southern*
Total Distance: *40 miles*
Total Elevation Gain: *1900 feet*
Type of Bike: *Road Bike*

Ride Rating: *Difficult*
Riding Time: *4 hours*
Calories Burned: *1200*

Terrain

The road has very little car traffic for the first 3.5 miles and even less beyond that. It is flat at first and then proceeds generally uphill.

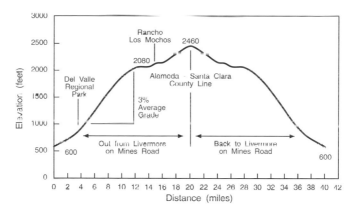

Ride Description

This out-and-back ride is very popular with the locals by virtue of its unique character as a country road with almost no traffic. After passing vineyards and farms, and then the turn-off for Del Valle Regional Park, it is quite common to ride for long periods of time without seeing any vehicles. The dramatic geography of the canyon seems out of place when one considers the nearness of the dense population centers of the Bay Area.

This ride takes you out 20 miles along Mines Road as it climbs to an elevation of nearly 2500 feet at the Santa Clara County line. The return back to Livermore is nearly all downhill. One of the nice features of an out-and-back ride is that you can come back at any point you wish and thus, you can tailor the ride to your own particular strength or time constraints. The truly aggressive rider can continue past the county line at

< Farm scene along San Ramon Boulevard

the 20-mile point all the way to the top of Mount Hamilton through the isolated San Antonio Valley.

Starting Point

Start the ride just out of Livermore, at the intersection of South Livermore Avenue and Mines Road. To get there, take Highway 580 and get off at the Livermore Avenue exit. Proceed south on Livermore Avenue for about 3½ miles to the intersection with Mines Road on the right side and park anywhere nearby.

Ride Details and Mile Markers

0.0   Proceed SOUTH on Mines Road.

3.5   Turn LEFT to stay on Mines Road. Del Valle Road continues straight ahead to Del Valle Regional Park, about 3 miles in on this road. At the park is a lake with swimming, boating, and fishing, and trails for hiking and cycling. There is a climb with about 800 feet of elevation gain before the road descends to the lake.

14.8   Rancho Los Mochos (Boy Scout Camp) on the right side.

20.1   Begin San Antonio Valley Road at the Santa Clara County line. Return back on Mines Road the way you came.

40.2   Back at the start point.

Remote country scene along Mines Road

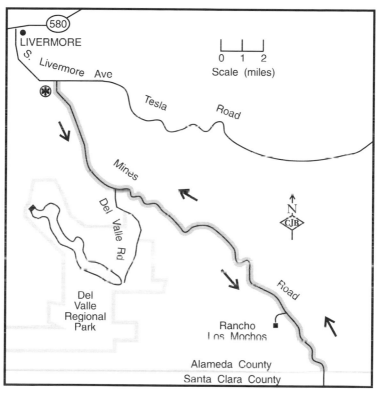

Ride No. 21

22 PLEASANTON
Tour of the Livermore Valley

Region: *Southern*
Total Distance: *26 miles*
Total Elevation Gain: *300 feet*
Type of Bike: *Road Bike*

Ride Rating: *Moderate*
Riding Time: *2-3 hours*
Calories Burned: *600*

Terrain

Although there is a gradual gain in elevation as the route heads toward Livermore, it is almost imperceptible. Bike lanes, wide roads and about 6 miles on multi-use paved trails make the ride quite safe.

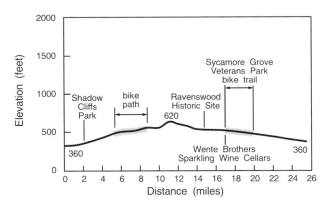

Ride Description

The charming and historic towns of Pleasanton and Livermore, the peaceful open countryside between and around them, and the many fine wineries dotting the countryside combine to give this ride a unique appeal for cyclists. Beginning in central Pleasanton, with its historic Kottinger's Barn and Pleasanton Hotel, the route leads to Livermore on a bike lane along busy Stanley Boulevard. Once on the outskirts of Livermore, a paved trail takes you through scenic residential areas and past some of the many vineyards of the Livermore Valley. The country roads around Livermore lead past the Wente Brothers and Concannon vineyards and tasting rooms and the Ravenswood Historic Site, where you can tour the restored mansion and grounds of one of the early settlers to the area. More rural roads lead to the dramatic architecture of the Wente Brothers Sparkling Wine Cellars, after which another paved trail passes through grassy fields and pastureland of Sycamore Grove

Park. The route back to Pleasanton is along Vineyard Avenue, with open fields dotted with trees and backed by the distant hills, ultimately giving way to modern residential subdivisions near town.

Starting Point

Start the ride in central Pleasanton, at the corner of Main Street and Neal Street. To get there, take Highway 680 to either the Bernal Road or Sunol Boulevard exits for Pleasanton. Proceed into Pleasanton and park anywhere near the downtown section.

Ride Details and Mile Markers

0.0 Proceed EAST on Main Street.

0.2 Historic Pleasanton Hotel on the left side.

0.3 Turn RIGHT onto Stanley Boulevard.

0.7 Turn LEFT to stay on Stanley Boulevard (1st Street intersects on the right side).

1.1 Get on the bike path parallel to the road on the right side.

2.0 Shadow Cliffs Regional Recreation Area entrance on the right side.

5.2 Turn RIGHT onto Murrieta Boulevard and then get on the bike path on the right side, just off the road.

5.8 Roadway underpass.

6.4 Roadway underpass.

6.5 Cross wooden bridge.

Courtesy of Wente Brothers Winery

7.4 Cross South Livermore Avenue and resume bike path on the far side. Retzlaff Vineyards and Concannon Vineyard on right side.

7.9 Cross Hillcrest Avenue and continue on bike path along Findlay Way.

8.2 Cross Madison Avenue and continue on bike path.

8.5 Turn LEFT onto Almond Avenue at the end of the bike path.

8.7 Turn RIGHT onto East Avenue.

9.8 Turn RIGHT onto South Vasco Road.

10.8 Turn RIGHT onto Tesla Road.

11.2 Wente Brothers winery on the left side.

11.6 Concannon Vineyards on the right side.

12.2 Turn LEFT onto Wente Street.

13.1 Road turns sharply to the right and becomes Marina Avenue.

14.2 Turn LEFT onto Arroyo Road.

14.4 Ravenswood Historic Site on the right side.

15.0 Wetmore Road intersection on the right side.

16.7 Wente Brothers Sparkling Wine Cellars on the left side.

17.0 Turn RIGHT into Sycamore Grove Veterans Park and proceed through parking lot to paved trail through the park.

17.3 Cross wooden bridge.

19.4 Turn LEFT onto Wetmore Road at the end of the paved trail.

19.7 Turn LEFT onto Vallecitos Road (Highway 84).

20.0 Turn RIGHT onto Vineyard Avenue.

24.3 Turn LEFT onto Bernal Avenue.

24.4 Turn RIGHT to get on the continuation of Vineyard Avenue.

25.1 Cross Stanley Boulevard and begin Ray Street.

25.4 Turn LEFT onto Main Street.

25.7 Back at the start point.

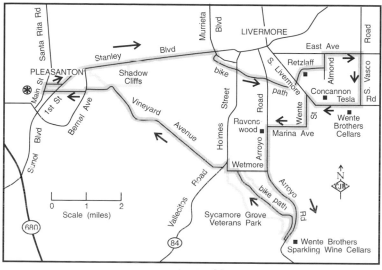

Ride No. 22

Ravenswood Historic Site in Livermore

23 PLEASANTON

Camino Tassajara and Collier Canyon Loop

	Ride 23A	Ride 23B
Region:	Southern	
Ride Rating:	Moderate	Moderate
Total Distance:	25 miles	31 miles
Riding Time:	2-3 hours	3-4 hours
Total Elevation Gain:	500 feet	600 feet
Calories Burned:	600	700
Type of Bike:	Road Bike	Road Bike

Ride Description

Charming Pleasanton is the start of this pair of rides over quiet country roads north of town. Site of the landmark Pleasanton Hotel and historic Kottinger's Barn, Pleasanton also is home to the Pleasanton Cheese Factory and numerous restaurants and shops. The countryside along each of these routes is dominated by farms and ranches, with the hillsides punctuated with trees and grazing livestock. Springtime is best, when the hills are green with fresh growth and the scent of wildflowers fills the crisp, clean air.

Starting Point

Start the ride in central Pleasanton, at the corner of Main Street and Neal Street. To get there, take Highway 680 to either the Bernal Road or Sunol Boulevard exits for Pleasanton. Proceed into Pleasanton and park anywhere near the downtown section.

Ride 23A (Moderate)

Leading east out of town toward Livermore, this route follows a bike path past Shadow Cliffs Recreation Area along busy Stanley Boulevard. In the outskirts of Livermore, you change direction to head north past the Livermore Airport and then into the countryside as you follow rural Collier Canyon Road. The ranches and pastureland along Highland Avenue continue as you return to Pleasanton along the gentle downhill grade of Camino Tassajara. Once over the freeway and into the outskirts of Pleasanton, busy city streets return you to your starting point.

Terrain

Country roads carry little traffic and rolling hills offer moderate challenge on this ride. Prevailing northerly winds gently push you back to Pleasanton on the return leg of the route.

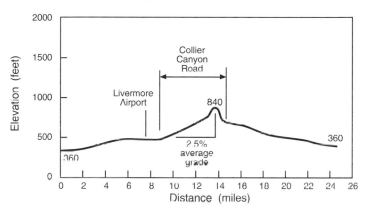

Ride 23A: Ride Details and Mile Markers

0.0 Proceed EAST on Main Street.

0.2 Historic Pleasanton Hotel on the left side.

0.3 Turn RIGHT onto Stanley Boulevard.

0.7 Turn LEFT to stay on Stanley Boulevard (1st Street intersects on the right side).

1.1 Get on the bike path parallel to the road on the right side.

2.0 Shadow Cliffs Regional Recreation Area entrance on the right side.

5.2 Turn LEFT onto Murrieta Boulevard.

6.0 Turn LEFT onto East Jack London Boulevard.

6.8 Turn RIGHT onto Kitty Hawk Road.

7.5 Road turns sharply to the right. Livermore Municipal Airport on the left side.

7.8 Highway 580 overpass.

8.0 Turn RIGHT onto North Canyons Parkway.

8.8 Turn LEFT onto Collier Canyon Road.

9.0 Las Positas College on the right side.

12.8 Carneal Road intersection on the right side.

13.7 Crest — 840 feet.

14.3 Turn LEFT onto Highland Road.

16.3 Turn LEFT onto Camino Tassajara.

21.8 Highway 580 overpass — begin Santa Rita Road.

24.3 Pleasanton Hotel on right side — begin Main Street.

24.6 Back at the start point.

Ride 23B (Moderate)

As in Ride 23A, this route follows Stanley Boulevard toward Livermore and heads north past Livermore Airport to rural Collier Canyon Road and then Highland Road. At this point, Ride 23B diverges from Ride 23A and leads north on Camino Tassajara. You pass more ranches and farms as you head toward the fashionable Blackhawk residential development built on the site of the former Blackhawk Ranch. Dougherty Road returns you to Pleasanton with a usual prevailing tailwind pushing you down a gentle slope back into town.

Terrain

This ride has two slight hills along lightly travelled roads. Morning is best if you want to avoid the afternoon headwinds coming in from the north.

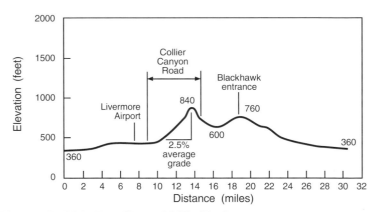

Ride 23B: Ride Details and Mile Markers

0.0 Proceed EAST on Main Street.

0.2 Historic Pleasanton Hotel on the left side.

0.3 Turn RIGHT onto Stanley Boulevard.

0.7 Turn LEFT to stay on Stanley Boulevard (1st Street intersects on the right side).

1.1 Get on the bike path parallel to the road on the right side.

2.0 Shadow Cliffs Regional Recreation Area entrance on the right side.

5.2 Turn LEFT onto Murrieta Boulevard.

6.0 Turn LEFT onto East Jack London Boulevard.

6.8 Turn RIGHT onto Kitty Hawk Road.

7.5 Road turns sharply to the right. Livermore Municipal Airport on the left side.

7.8 Highway 580 overpass.

8.0 Turn RIGHT onto North Canyons Parkway.

8.8 Turn LEFT onto Collier Canyon Road.
9.0 Las Positas College on the right side.
12.8 Carneal Road intersection on the right side.
13.7 Crest — 840 feet.
14.3 Turn LEFT onto Highland Road.
16.3 Turn RIGHT onto Camino Tassajara.
18.7 East entrance to Blackhawk on right side.
21.0 Turn LEFT onto Crow Canyon Road.
21.8 Turn LEFT onto Dougherty Road.
27.0 Cross Dublin Boulevard.
27.2 Highway 580 overpass — begin Hopyard Road.
29.1 Pleasanton Sports Park on the left side.
29.9 Begin Division Street.
30.5 Turn RIGHT onto Main Street.
30.6 Back at the start point.

Pleasanton Hotel

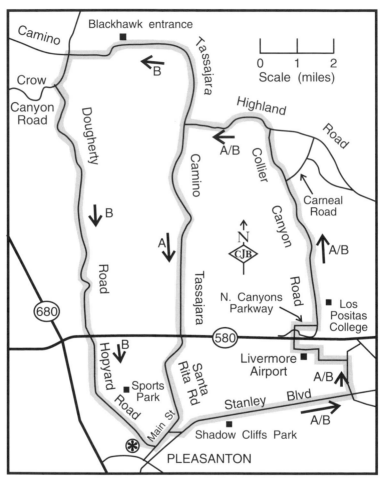

Ride Nos. 23A and 23B

24 FREMONT
Alameda Creek Trail and Mission San José

Region: *Southern*
Total Distance: *18 miles*
Total Elevation Gain: *400 feet*
Type of Bike: *Road Bike*

Ride Rating: *Easy*
Riding Time: *2 hours*
Calories Burned: *450*

Terrain

This ride is generally flat, along city streets with two small hills in the latter half. It includes about 3 miles on loose gravel along Alameda Creek Regional Trail, a multi-use pathway following Alameda Creek. The trail is smooth and the stones are small, so road bikes work fine.

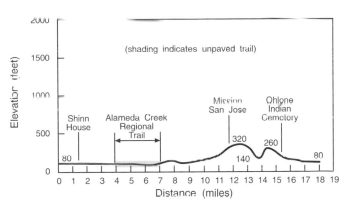

Ride Description

Central Park, a large recreational area in central Fremont, is the starting point for the ride. Restrooms and water are available there and the park is a nice spot for a picnic following the ride. Leading out of the park through quiet residential neighborhoods, the route takes you past Shinn Historic Park, site of the restored Victorian home of James Shinn, an early California pioneer. Built in 1876, the home is today open to the public and furnished with period pieces, including some mementos of the Shinn family. After crossing Alameda Creek, you head back toward Fremont along Alameda Creek Regional Trail, which you share with pedestrians and runners. Bikes must yield to others at all times.

Canyon Heights Drive and Morrison Canyon Road lead to Mission Boulevard, a busy thoroughfare with a wide bike lane for safety. There is a gentle climb along Mission Boulevard as it takes you past Mission

San José, a fine example of early California missions. Originally founded in 1797, the mission built its church in 1805. After it was completely destroyed in a massive earthquake in 1868, a wooden church occupied the site until 1965, when it was moved to another location to make way for the current structure, a replica of the original. The adjacent cemetery contains the graves of many of the early pioneers of the region.

Durham Road and Paseo Padre Boulevard lead through residential areas and over a short, but steep hill, back to Central Park, from where you started.

Starting Point

Start the ride in Fremont, in Central Park on Stevenson Boulevard, at the park entrance at Gallaudet Drive. To get there from Highway 880, take the Stevenson Boulevard exit and proceed east on Stevenson Boulevard about 2½ miles. From Highway 680, get off at the exit for Mission Boulevard (there are two Mission Boulevard exits, so look for the one for Ohlone College). Follow Mission Boulevard north and turn left onto Stevenson Boulevard. Park near the tennis courts in the park.

Ride Details and Mile Markers

0.0 Proceed out of the park across Stevenson Boulevard and onto Gallaudet Drive.

0.4 Cross Walnut Avenue and begin Cherry Lane.

1.0 Turn LEFT onto Mowry Avenue.

1.3 Bear RIGHT to get on Peralta Boulevard. Shinn Historic Park on the right side just after the turn.

2.3 Turn RIGHT onto Paseo Padre parkway.

3.8 Turn RIGHT onto Isherwood Way.

3.9 Turn RIGHT onto Alameda Creek Regional Trail just after crossing over bridge on Isherwood Way.

4.7 Alameda Creek Quarries Recreation Area visible on the left side.

5.4 Continue on trail as it passes under railroad tracks.

6.5 Continue on trail as it passes under second railroad tracks.

6.6 Cross Mission Boulevard to get on the continuation of the trail.

6.9 End of the trail — turn RIGHT onto Old Canyon Road.

7.3 Turn RIGHT onto Clark Drive and then turn RIGHT again onto Canyon Heights Drive.

8.2 Turn RIGHT onto Morrison Canyon Road.

8.5 Turn LEFT onto Mission Boulevard.

11.2 Highway 680 underpass.

11.7 Mission San José on the left side.

11.9 Ohlone College on the left side.

13.1 Turn RIGHT onto Durham Road.

13.8 Turn RIGHT onto Paseo Padre Parkway.

15.3 Ohlone Indian Cemetery on the left side on Washington Boulevard. Not open to the public.

15.5 Highway 680 overpass.

17.3 Turn RIGHT into Central Park at Grimmer Boulevard intersection, on the left side. Continue through the parking lot to get on the paved pathway in the park. Follow the pathway around the right side of the lake to the far end of the park, the place at which you started.

18.2 Back at the start point.

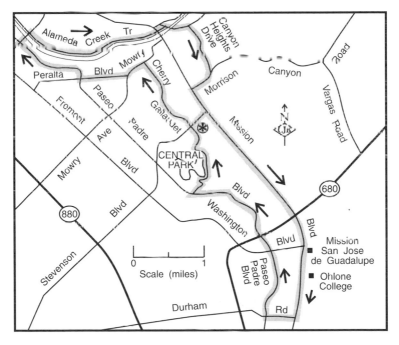

Ride No. 24

25 FREMONT
Calaveras Road Ride

Region: *Southern*
Total Distance: *38 miles*
Total Elevation Gain: *1500 feet*
Type of Bike: *Road Bike*

Ride Rating: *Difficult*
Riding Time: *3-4 hours*
Calories Burned: *1100*

Terrain

A long, isolated stretch along Calaveras Road, with a sustained hill climb, is free of traffic. In contrast, a large part of the route, along Warm Springs Boulevard, Mission Boulevard and Niles Canyon Road, is very busy and extra caution is advised.

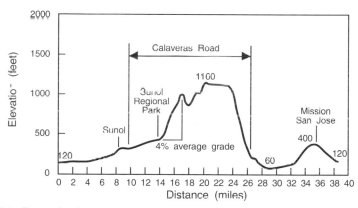

Ride Description

Beginning in Fremont, the route leads north along Mission Boulevard and cuts across to Niles Canyon Road through quiet residential areas. Niles Canyon Road is narrow and very busy, so it is important to be very careful and to always ride as far to the right as possible.

Just past the tiny town of Sunol, after crossing under the freeway, remote Calaveras Road begins. Traffic will be light as this road takes you into isolated areas very different from the heavily populated cities of the East Bay. As the road climbs over a long and steady grade, sweeping views of the Sunol Regional Wilderness come into view with its dramatic rock formations at the top of the hills across the valley. As you ride along the crest for about 3 miles, Calaveras Reservoir is visible below.

< Mission San José de Guadalupe

The steep and winding descent takes you past Ed Levin County Park and onto the busy residential and commercial streets of Milpitas. The return to Fremont along North Milpitas Boulevard, Warm Springs Boulevard and Mission Boulevard carries lots of traffic, but has wide bike lanes for your safety. Be sure to stop at Mission San José for a tour of one of the early California missions and learn about its historic past.

Starting Point

Start the ride in Fremont, in Central Park on Stevenson Boulevard, at the park entrance at Gallaudet Drive. To get there from Highway 880, take the Stevenson Boulevard exit and proceed east on Stevenson Boulevard about 2½ miles. From Highway 680, exit at Mission Boulevard (there are two Mission Boulevard exits, so look for the one for Ohlone College). Follow Mission Boulevard north and turn left onto Stevenson Boulevard. Park near the tennis courts in the park.

Ride Details and Mile Markers

0.0   Proceed EAST on Stevenson Boulevard, toward Mission Boulevard.

0.3   Turn LEFT onto Mission Boulevard.

0.8   Turn RIGHT onto Morrison Canyon Road.

1.1   Turn LEFT onto Canyon Heights Road.

1.9   Turn LEFT onto Clark Drive and then LEFT onto Old Canyon Road.

2.3   Turn RIGHT onto Niles Canyon Road (Highway 84).

3.5   Cross under railroad trestle.

8.4   Turn RIGHT to exit the highway at Sunol. Pass through Sunol to avoid the narrow section of Niles Canyon Road. In Sunol there is a small grocery store.

8.8   Turn LEFT back onto Niles Canyon Road.

8.9   Bear RIGHT at the stop sign to stay on Niles Canyon Road. Down the road to the right is the Hetch Hetchy Water Temple.

9.7   Highway 680 underpass and begin Calaveras Road.

14.0 Geary Road intersection on the left side, the entrance for Sunol Regional Wilderness. Begin climbing.

17.5 Calaveras Dam and Reservoir visible in the distance to the left.

20.1 Crest — 1160 feet.

23.7 Begin steep descent.

23.9 Bear RIGHT at stop sign to stay on Calaveras Road. Felter Road is on the left side.

24.8 Ed R. Levin County Park headquarters on the left side and golf course on the right side.

26.4 Turn RIGHT onto Evans Road.

27.6 Begin Jacklin Road.

27.8 Highway 680 underpass.

28.7 Turn RIGHT onto North Milpitas Boulevard.

30.0 Enter Fremont and begin Warm Springs Boulevard.

32.1 Turn RIGHT onto Mission Boulevard.

32.6 Highway 680 underpass.

34.8 Ohlone College on the right side.

35.4 Mission San José on the right side.

35.9 Highway 680 underpass.

38.1 Railroad underpass, then turn LEFT onto Stevenson Boulevard.

38.4 Back at the start point.

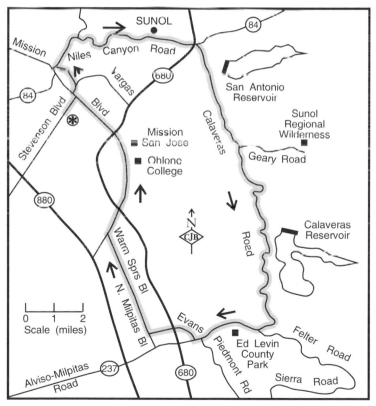

Ride No. 25

26 SUNOL
Pleasanton Ridge Mountain Bike Ride

Region: *Southern*
Total Distance: *9 miles*
Total Elevation Gain: *1600 feet*
Type of Bike: *Mountain Bike*

Ride Rating: *Difficult*
Riding Time: *2 hours*
Calories Burned: *900*

Terrain

Following wide fire roads, this ride has plenty of very steep terrain. Even along the crest, expect to shift gears frequently as you go up and down steep slopes.

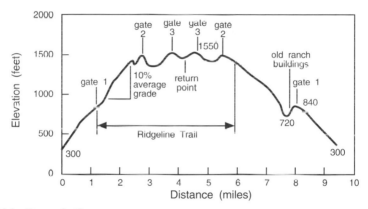

Ride Description

Leaving the parking area on Oak Tree Trail, the route climbs immediately toward the intersection with Ridgeline Trail. Grassy slopes and oak dotted hillsides are the dominant features of the park as Ridgeline Trail continues its climb skyward. Along the ridge, panoramic vistas east into the Livermore Valley and beyond come into view and a conveniently placed picnic table beckons you to rest and to savor the moment.

The open landscape of Ridgeline Trail changes abruptly as you pass through a heavily wooded section just before getting back on Ridgeline Trail. The return is initially back along Ridgeline Trail and then along Thermalito Trail, with views of the west side of the ridge and Kilkare Canyon, far below. After passing some old ranch buildings, you descend back to the parking lot along Oak Tree Trail.

Starting Point

Start the ride at the entrance for Pleasanton Regional Park on Foothill Road, just north of Sunol. To get there, take Highway 680 toward Pleasanton and get off at Bernal Avenue. Proceed west on Bernal Avenue for a short distance and then south on Foothill Road for about 3 miles to Pleasanton Ridge Regional Park, where there is plenty of parking.

Ride Details and Mile Markers

0.0   Proceed out of the parking area away from the road on Oak Tree Trail.

0.6   Continue STRAIGHT at intersection with trail to Sycamore Groves on the right side.

1.2   Turn RIGHT and pass through gate on Oak Tree Trail, then turn RIGHT again to get on Ridgeline Trail and begin steep climb.

1.4   Bear RIGHT to stay on Ridgeline Trail.

1.8   Olive Trail intersection on the left side.

2.3   Trail toward Thermalito Trail on the left side.

2.5   Thermalito Trail intersection on the left side.

2.8   Continue past gate, then bear RIGHT to stay on Ridgeline Trail. Steep downhill section.

2.9   Turn LEFT to stay on Ridgeline Trail.

3.1   Enter Augustine Bernal Park area.

3.7   Continue past gate and turn RIGHT onto unmarked trail. This will ultimately re-connect to Ridgeline Trail.

4.2   Turn LEFT onto Ridgeline Trail and head back.

4.6   Continue past gate and stay on Ridgeline Trail.

5.5   Continue past gate.

5.9   Turn RIGHT onto Thermalito Trail.

7.7   Turn LEFT onto Oak Tree Trail.

7.8   Pass by old ranch buildings.

8.0   Continue STRAIGHT across Ridgeline Trail, pass gate, and turn LEFT to stay on Oak Tree Trail.

9.4   Back at the start point.

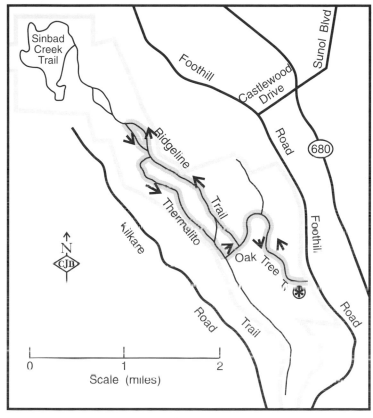

Ride No. 26

Ridgeline Trail

27 **NEWARK**

Coyote Hills Mountain Bike Ride

Region: *Southern*
Total Distance: *15 miles*
Total Elevation Gain: *100 feet*
Type of Bike: *Mountain Bike*

Ride Rating: *Easy*
Riding Time: *2 hours*
Calories Burned: *300*

Terrain

The ride is very flat along mostly paved trails, except for some stretches on loose gravel. A mountain bike is suggested, but a road bike with sturdy tires will work fine.

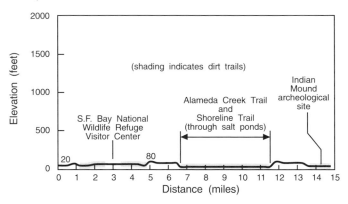

Ride Description

Home to Ohlone Indians for over 2000 years, Coyote Hills is today a unique place to experience the wetlands of San Francisco Bay. Ringed with a network of hiking and biking trails, the grassy hillsides of the park stand out against the flat low-lying land all around. The marshes and mudflats along the coastline are home to the many insects and marine animals, which serve as the food supply for the wide variety of birds frequently seen in the park.

This route takes you into the park and immediately heads south along the shore of the bay toward the San Francisco Bay National Wildlife Refuge, where you can get off your bike and explore the wetlands and tour the informative visitor center there. Back at Coyote Hills, the route leads north along Bayview Trail and then out into the bay along the Alameda Creek Regional Trail. Riding along the Shoreline Trail past the salt ponds, you can experience the magnificence of the bay while you view the Dumbarton Bridge in the distance. The return to the park puts you again on the

Bayview Trail as it follows the shoreline. Through the marshes and past the Indian Mound Archaeological Site, you return to the parking lot.

Starting Point

Start the ride at the parking lot at the entrance to Coyote Hills Regional Park. To get there, take Highway 880 to Newark and get off at the exit for Highway 84. Head west on Highway 84, toward the Dumbarton Bridge and exit at Ardenwood Boulevard. Proceed north on Ardenwood Boulevard, turn left onto Paseo Padre Parkway, right onto Patterson Ranch Road, and follow this road into Coyote Hills Park.

Ride Details and Mile Markers

0.0   Proceed WEST out of the parking area into Coyote Hills Regional Park on the paved trail that runs parallel to the roadway.

0.4   Turn LEFT onto Bayview Trail and cross the road.

0.9   Bear LEFT to stay on paved trail.

1.1   Bear RIGHT toward Shoreline Trail and Apay Way.

1.2   Turn LEFT onto San Francisco Bay Trail (Apay Way) — dirt trail.

2.4   Operating quarry on left side.

2.6   Cross Highway 84 on bridge overpass.

3.0   San Francisco Bay National Wildlife Refuge visitor center. Be sure to stop for a visit and a walk through the wetlands. When you are finished, return the way you came.

4.8   Turn LEFT back onto paved Bayview Trail.

6.5   Turn LEFT toward Alameda Creek and then turn LEFT again onto Alameda Creek Regional Trail, heading west toward the bay — unpaved trail.

8.7   Begin Shoreline Trail in S.F. Bay National Wildlife Refuge. Dumbarton Bridge is visible ahead.

Bayview Trail

9.6   Continue STRAIGHT toward Coyote Hills. Shoreline Trail turns to the right at this point.

11.5   Turn LEFT onto paved Bayview Trail back in Coyote Hills Regional Park.

13.2   Continue STRAIGHT on Bayview Trail at the point where Alameda Creek Trail access is to the left.

13.6   Turn LEFT onto Lizard Rock Trail toward Chochenyo Trail.

13.8   Turn LEFT onto unmarked trail.

14.0   Turn RIGHT onto unmarked trail through the marsh and then turn LEFT onto Chochenyo Trail toward Indian Mound.

14.3   Turn RIGHT to go around the Indian Mound archaeological site — closed to the public.

14.4   Bear RIGHT at the far end of the site.

14.8   Back at the parking lot.

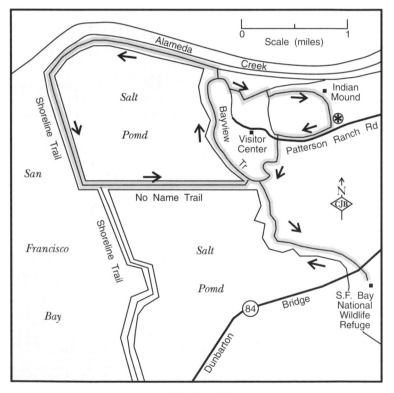

Ride No. 27

APPENDIX

RIDES BY RATINGS

Easy Rides
(short rides, easy grades, for beginners and children)

Moderate Rides
(longer rides, some hills, not too strenuous)

Difficult Rides
(long rides with strenuous grades, for advanced cyclists)

MOUNTAIN BIKE RIDES

North Gate Road in Mount Diablo State Park

BICYCLE SHOPS IN THE EAST BAY

Alameda

Alameda Bicycle
1522 Park Street
(510) 522-0070

Joe's Bike Shop
1408 Encinal Avenue
(510) 523-9857

The Pedaler
883-C Island Drive
(510) 865-3400

Stone's Cyclery
2320 Santa Clara Ave
(510) 523-3264

Albany

Solano Avenue Cyclery
1554 Solano Avenue
(510) 524-1094

Antioch

Antioch Cyclery
611 West 9th
(510) 778-4898

Schwinn City
814 A Street
(510) 757-0664

Berkeley

*Ashby Avenue Bike
Doctors*
1945 Ashby Avenue
(510) 843-1427

*Backroads Bicycle Shop
& Warehouse*
801 Cedar Street
(510) 527-1888

*Berkeley Cycle &
Fitness*
2020 Center Street
(510) 845-7560

Jitensha Studio
2250 Bancroft Way
(510) 540-6240

Karim Cyclery
2801 Telegraph Ave
(510) 843-7471

The Missing Link
1988 Shattuck Avenue
(510) 843-7471

Pacific Bicycle
2701 College Avenue
(510) 644-3751

REI
1338 San Pablo Ave
(510) 527-4140

The Square Wheel
1347 ML King Jr Way
(510) 527-5682

Velo Sports Bicycles
1650 ML King Jr Way
(510) 849-0437

Brentwood

East County Cycles
71 Sand Creek Road
(510) 634-8969

Castro Valley

Castro Valley Cyclepath
3418 Castro Vly Blvd
(510) 538-2062

Castro Valley Cyclery
20664 Santa Maria
(510) 538-1878

Concord

*Clayton Valley Bicycle
Center*
5400 Ygnacio Vly Rd
(510) 672-2522

Concord Cyclery
3561 Clayton Road
(510) 687-8148

John's Used Bicycles
2836 Clayton Road
(510) 798-8483

Danville

California Pedaler
295 South Hartz Ave
(510) 820-0345

Danville Bike
379 North Hartz Ave
(510) 837-0966

Dublin

Dublin Cyclery
7381 Amador Vly Blvd
(510) 828-8676

El Cerrito

*El Cerrito Cycle &
Fitness*
10400 San Pablo Ave
(510) 524-8810

El Sobrante

El Sobrante Schwinn
5057 El Portal Drive
(510) 223-3440

The Pedaler
3820A San Pablo Dam
Road
(510) 222-3420

Fremont

CAL Bicycles
46529 Mission Blvd
(510) 490-3333

F&M Cyclery
39030 Argonaut Way
(510) 793-0566

Fremont Schwinn
4040 Papazian Way
(510) 656-8610

Mission Cyclery
43362 Bryant Street
(510) 656-6000

Niles Ski & Bike
37469 Niles Blvd
(510) 793-9141

Tri-City Sporting Goods
40900 Grimmer Blvd
(510) 651-9600

Hayward

Cyclepath
22510 Foothill Blvd
(510) 881-5177

Hank & Frank Bicycles
933 C Street
(510) 582-6118

Witt's Bicycle Shop
22125 Mission Blvd
(510) 538-8771

Lafayette

Hank & Frank Bicycles
3377 Mt. Diablo Blvd
(510) 283-2453

Lafayette Cycleworks
3422 Mt. Diablo Blvd
(510) 284-1700

Livermore

Livermore Cycle Center
2133 First Street
(510) 447-6666

Livermore Cyclery
2288 First Street
(510) 455-8090

Martinez

The Cyclery Group
4990 Pacheco Blvd
(510) 228-9277

Milpitas

Paramount Cyclery &
Sports
12 North Abel Street
(408) 945-6580

Spectrum Cycles
1402 Dempsey Road
(408) 946-3746

Town & Country Bicycles
1257 Jacklin Road
(408) 946-8501

Moraga

The Bicycle Connection
554 Center Street
(510) 376-6060

Newark

Bike Threads
39269 Cedar Blvd
(510) 713-7911

Newark Schwinn Cyclery
35201 Newark Blvd
(510) 793-4546

Oakland

Carl's Bikes
2416 Telegraph Ave
(510) 835-8763

Hank & Frank Bicycles
6030 College Avenue
(510) 658-1177

Pioneer Bike Shop
11 Rio Vista Avenue
(510) 658-8981

Montclair Sports
1970 Mountain Blvd
(510) 339-9313

Sam & Rick's Bicycles
106 East 14th Street
(510) 451-6245

Oakley

DeltaFreewheeler
699 Main Street
(510) 625-8200

Orinda

Orinda Spoke & Pedal
17 Orinda Way
(510) 254-1575

Pinole

Pinole Valley Schwinn
2830 Pinole Valley Rd
(510) 758-2433

Pleasant Hill

Contra Costa Cyclery
2263 Contra Costa Blvd
(510) 676-2666

Pleasanton

California Pedaler
525 Main Street
(510) 462-9777

Paquette's Cyclery
1987 Santa Rita Road
(510) 846-4788

Sam & Rick's Bicycles
3510 Old Santa Rita Rd
(510) 847-0666

Richmond

Sharp Bicycle
2800 Hilltop Mall Rd
(510) 222-8004

San Leandro

M & J Bicycle Shop
16884 East 14th Street
(510) 276-1132

Marina Bike Works
10 San Leandro Marina
(510) 483-4495

Robinson Wheel Works
1255 MacArthur Blvd
(510) 352-4663

Ross Bicycles
142 Greenhouse
Marketplace
(510) 352-7777

San Leandro Schwinn
471 East 14th Street
(510) 633-2453

San Lorenzo

Movin' On Cyclery
18050 Hesperian Blvd
(510) 276-5660

San Ramon

Any Mountain Bikes
490 Market Place
(510) 275-1010

San Ramon Cyclery
12171 Alcosta Blvd
(510) 833-1825

STD Cycle
2550 San Ramon Vly
Blvd
(510) 820-2998

Walnut Creek

Diablo Bike
2040 Mt. Diablo Blvd
(510) 932-2323

Encina Bicycle Center
2891 Ygnacio Valley Rd
(510) 944-9200

Bike-in-a-Box Cyclery
of Walnut Creek
2635 North Main St.
(510) 935-3131

Octopus Bicycles
1500 Sunnyvale Ave
(510) 935-6001

Tandems of Walnut Creek
2065 San Miguel Dr
(510) 937-2453

Walnut Creek Cyclery
1291 Parkside Drive
(510) 930-7012

CYCLING CLUBS AND ORGANIZATIONS IN THE EAST BAY

Berkeley Bicycle Club
Box 817, Berkeley 94701
Ken Rodriguez (510) 525-6473
Racing and training for competitive cyclists

Berkeley Trip Commute Store
2033 Center Street, Berkeley 94704
(510) 644-7665
Bike maps, carpool and transit information

Bicycle Trails Council of the East Bay
Box 9583, Berkeley 94709
(510) 528-BIKE
Mountain Biking and trail advocacy group

Big O Bicycle Club, Walnut Creek
Otto Noack (510) 935-0624
Casual group riding and serious training

CAL Cycling Club
2301 Bancroft #210, Berkeley 94720
(510) 486-1760
UCSF racing club

Cherry City Cyclists
Box 1972, San Leandro 94577
Mike Van Alstyne (510) 483-7315
Recreational cycling and touring

Coast Range Riders, East Bay
Matt (510) 222-8004
Hotline: (510) 653-6383
Off-road cycling club

The Cyclery Group, Contra Costa County
John Lewis (510) 930-7012
Recreational rides, maintenance classes, training

Devil Mountain Cyclists
Box 4381, Walnut Creek 94596
(510) 672-IDMC
Racing and training

East Bay Bicycle Coalition
Box 1736, Oakland 94604
(510) 452-1221
Advocacy group for cycling for transportation and recreation

East County Cyclists, Eastern Contra Costa County
Box 331, Antioch 94509
Mike McKnelly (510) 778-6706
Touring and mountain biking

Fremont Freewheelers, Southern Alameda County
Box 1089, Fremont 94538
Scott Campbell (510) 656-0511
Touring, recreation, UCSF racing

Grizzly Peak Cyclists
Box 9308, Berkeley 94709
Alan Forkosh (510) 655-6221
Recreational cycling

LLLRA Cycletrons
Lawrence Livermore National Laboratory
Box 808, L-333, Livermore 94550
Steve Benson (510) 423-7448
Lunchtime rides

Milpitas Cyclists, Milpitas
Charles (510) 251-2250
Fast-paced Sunday rides

Northern California Triathlon Club
c/o Golden Triangle Athletic Club
2033 No. Main St, Walnut Creek 94596
(510) 730-7900
Training and seminars for all levels and ages

Oakland Yellowjackets, Oakland
Rene or Leo (510) 835-8763
Beginning and advanced group rides

Stockton Bicycle Club
Box 4702, Stockton 95204
Lanna King (209) 759-3571

Team Pedaler, East Bay Area
(510) 222-3420
Racing and training rides

Valley Spokesmen Bicycle Touring Club
Box 2630, Dublin 94568
Bonnie Powers (510) 828-5299
Bicycle touring

CYCLING EVENTS IN THE EAST BAY

RECREATIONAL RIDES

Cinderella Classic *(Women only)*
Time of year: April
Place: Dublin
Sponsor: Valley Spokesmen
Information: (510) 828-5299

Livermore Fitness Day
Time of year: April
Place: Livermore
Information: (510) 373-5700

Primavera Century
Time of year: April
Place: Fremont
Sponsor: Fremont Free-
wheelers Bike Club
Information: Barry Parks
(510) 656-8128

Delta Century
Time of year: May
Place: Stockton
Sponsor: Stockton Bicycle Club
Information: (209) 759-3571

Grizzly Peak Century
Time of year: May
Place: Berkeley
Sponsor: Grizzly Peak Cyclists
Information: (510) 655-6221

Hekaton Classic
Time of year: September
Place: Dublin
Sponsor: Valley Spokesmen
Information: (510) 455-4677

Cheery City Jubilee Century
Time of year: September
Place: Livermore
Sponsor: Cherry City Cyclists
Information: (510) 483-7315

Benefit Rides

Mountain Challenge
Benefits: Children's Hospital,
Lafayette
Time of year: September
Place: Danville
Information: (510) 284-4343

San Ramon Valley Bike Adventure
Time of year: April
Place: Oak Hill Park,
Danville
Information: (510) 935-0472

RACES

Mount Diablo Classic
Triathlon/Run/Mountain Bike Race
Time of year: October
Place: Mount Diablo
State Park, Danville
Information: (510) 841-1190

PERIODIC PUBLICATIONS

California Bicyclist,
San Francisco
(510) 546-7291
Monthly, except February.
Includes listing of organized rides
and clubs. Available free at most
bike shops.

POINTS OF INTEREST

STATE PARKS

Mount Diablo State Park
 P.O. Box 250, Diablo 94528
 (510) 837-2525

FEATURED EAST BAY REGIONAL PARKS

c/o East Bay Regional Park District
 11500 Skyline Boulevard,
 Oakland 94629
 (510) 531-9300

Briones Regional Park
 Bear Creek Road, near Lafayette

Carquinez Strait Regional Shoreline
 Carquinez Scenic Drive,
 between Crockett and Martinez

Anthony Chabot Regional Park
 Lake Chabot Road, near San Leandro

Coyote Hills Regional Park
 Patterson Ranch Road, Newark

Contra Loma Regional Park
 Empire Mine Road, Antioch

Pleasanton Ridge Regional Park
 Foothill Road, Pleasanton

Redwood Regional Park
 Redwood Road, near San Leandro

Tilden and Wildcat Canyon Regional Parks
 Wildcat Canyon Road,
 Berkeley Hills

SELECTED WINERIES

Concannon Vineyard
 4590 Tesla Road, Livermore
 (510) 447-3760

Fenestra Winery
 83 East Vallecitos Road,
 Livermore
 (510) 447-5246

Livermore Valley Cellars
 1508 Wetmore Road, Livermore
 (510) 447-1751

Retzlaff Vineyards
 1356 South Livermore Ave,
 Livermore
 (510) 447-8941

Viano Vineyards
 150 Morello Avenue, Martinez
 (510) 228-6465

Weibel Vineyards
 1250 Stanford Avenue, Mission
 San Jose
 (510) 656-2340

Wente Brothers
 5565 Tesla Road, Livermore
 (510) 447-3603

MISCELLANEOUS

John Muir National Historic Site
 Alhambra Avenue
 at Highway 4, Martinez
 (510) 228-8860
 *Former home of the noted
 naturalist and founder of the
 Sierra Club.*

Lawrence Livermore National Laboratories
 Greenville Road at East
 Avenue, Livermore
 (510) 422-9797
 *Designs, manufactures, and
 tests all U.S. nuclear weapons.
 Visitor center with informative
 displays.*

CALIFORNIA BICYCLE LAWS

Excerpted from the 1990 California Vehicle Code, the following descriptions explain laws which pertain to cyclists.

RIGHTS AND RESPONSIBILITIES   21200

A. Bicyclists must obey all the laws which apply to operators of motor vehicles.

B. You must never ride under the influence of alcohol or drugs.

EQUIPMENT REQUIREMENTS   21201

A. You must have operating brakes.

B. Handlebars must not be elevated above the shoulders.

C. The size of the bicycle must not be so large that the operator cannot support the bike in an upright position with at least one foot on the ground.

D. When riding at night, the bicycle must be equipped with a front light, a rear reflector, pedal reflectors and reflectors on the front wheels visible from the sides.

OPERATION ON ROADWAY   21202

A. You must ride as far to the right of the roadway unless you are passing another vehicle, making a left turn, or avoiding hazardous road conditions.

B. On a one-way street, you may ride on the left side if you are as far to the left as practical.

HITCHING RIDES   21203

No person riding a bicycle is permitted to attach the bike or himself to any moving vehicle.

RIDING ON BICYCLE   21204

A. Bike must be equipped with a permanent and upright seat.

B. You may not ride as a passenger unless the bike is equipped with a separate seat. Seats for children must have adequate means of holding the child in place and for protection from moving parts on the bike.

C. Children riding as passengers must wear an ANSI-approved helmet.

BICYCLE LANES   21208

A. You must ride in designated bicycle lanes unless you are passing another vehicle in the lane, making a left turn, or avoiding hazardous obstacles.

B. You must give clear signals and operate with reasonable safety before you may leave a designated bike lane.

BICYCLE PARKING   21210

You may not leave your bicycle on a sidewalk in a way that impedes pedestrian traffic.

HAND SIGNALS   21211

It is required for bicyclists to signal turns and sudden changes in speed.

Left turn signal — left hand and arm fully extended and horizontal.

Right turn signal — left hand and arm extended to the left and the forearm pointing upward.

Slowing or stopping — the left hand and arm extended downward and the palm open-faced to the rear.

FREEWAYS   21960

You must obey signs which indicate freeways or expressways on which bicycle traffic is forbidden.

Marshland in Coyote Hills Regional Park

BICYCLING TIPS

Benefit from the experience of others by familiarizing yourself with these simple tips for better and safer cycling.

GENERAL RULES OF THE ROAD

1. Always ride on the right and never ride against the flow of traffic. Remember that bicycles are subject to the same driving rules as cars.

2. Keep as far to the right as possible in order to allow cars plenty of room to pass. Always ride in a single file.

3. Signal when you are turning or slowing down in order to allow the rider behind you to prepare for the same and to allow cars to know what you are doing. Never act suddenly, except in an absolute emergency.

4. Never ride on freeways. This is simply too dangerous.

5. Cross railroad tracks and cattle guards at right angles to the rails.

6. In the rain or on wet surfaces, ride slower and more cautiously than you normally would. Remember that not only are the roads wet, but so are your brakes.

7. Avoid night riding. If you absolutely must, be sure to wear highly visible clothing and carry a light.

8. Never assume that a car or another cyclist will give you the right of way. Always ride cautiously and defensively.

9. Be extra cautious when passing parked cars. Watch for doors to suddenly open.

10. Avoid riding on sidewalks, unless signs indicate that bicycles are permitted.

11. When making a left turn in traffic, ride assertively and give clear signals. Be sure to wave appreciatively when another vehicle gives you clearance.

12. Always stop at red lights and stop signs. Cyclists have no special privileges.

13. Signal to trailing cyclists the presence of debris or potholes in the road, either of which can be difficult for them to see.

RULES FOR OFF-ROAD BIKING

1. Know the rules for the area in which you are riding. Always stay on the trails intended for bikes. Leave the area just as you found it.

2. Yield to equestrians. Horses may spook when a bicycle appears suddenly.

3. Yield to hikers. Remember that they had use of the trails first.

4. Always be courteous. Nothing is worse for the sport than ill-will created by impolite actions.

5. Look ahead to anticipate encounters with others.

6. Avoid contact with plant life along the trails. Poison oak is very common in northern California and can be a very unpleasant experience.

7. Carry maps at all times. Getting lost is no fun.

TIPS ON YOUR EQUIPMENT

1. Always carry a spare tube, patch kit, tire pump and tools.

2. Be prepared to fix your own bike. Don't count on others to do this for you.

3. Check your equipment before you go, not after you are underway. Check tire pressure, seat height, brakes and shifters.

4. Tire pressure is usually indicated on the side of the tire. Mountain biking over rough or soft surfaces often works better when the tires are slightly deflated. Road riding requires fully inflated tires for maximum efficiency.

5. Carry adequate water supplies. This is especially true on hot days or when you are riding in areas with no services along the way.

6. A handlebar pack or panniers are convenient for carrying extra clothing or snacks.

7. Equip your bike with reflectors. They don't add much weight and they make it easier for others to see you.

8. Toe clips give you better riding efficiency on long rides. Mountain bikes are probably better without them, however, since you often need to dismount quickly in rough terrain.

9. A rear view mirror is a useful accessory and will permit you to see approaching riders and vehicles without turning around. This is especially useful if you ride with groups and want to keep track of trailing riders.

10. A chain and lock are recommended if you anticipate leaving your bike unattended and out of view.

APPROPRIATE CLOTHING

1. A helmet is mandatory. Your head is a very important part of your body and is very vulnerable without protection.

2. Wear bright clothing. You want to be easily seen by vehicle drivers.

3. Lycra shorts are not absolutely necessary, but offer more comfort on long rides. The constant rubbing of loose fitting shorts will be an annoyance and may cause a skin irritation.

4. Gloves are not necessary, but long rides without them can cause blisters or blood circulation problems.

5. Bicycling shoes with clip-in pedals are usually useful only for competitive riders. Most recreational cyclists often have difficulty engaging the pedals or in releasing from them when it becomes necessary to dismount quickly. Furthermore, it is difficult to walk with these shoes.

6. It is good to carry a lightweight windbreaker, even on warm days. High altitudes are often colder than you anticipate. Furthermore, if you perspire a lot on an uphill climb, you may want to put on the windbreaker for the descent.

7. Long pants and winter gloves are usually necessary for rides in the cold months.

8. Some sort of eyewear is strongly recommended. Either cycling goggles or sunglasses will provide protection from dirt, debris and insects, as well as screen your eyes from the harmful effects of the sun's ultraviolet rays.

TECHNIQUES

1. A properly adjusted seat height will ensure you comfort and will help to avoid knee injuries. The correct height will result in a slight bend in the knee when the leg is in its fully extended position to the lower of the two pedals.

2. Be familiar with gear shifting so you can anticipate hill climbs and shift before you need to. It is difficult to shift when there is a lot of pressure on the pedals. Always shift while you are pedaling to ensure that the chain does not come off.

3. The upright position (on dropped handlebars) is usually most comfortable for the majority of road riding. Position yourself on the lower bars to reduce your wind resistance on downhill runs and to get maximum leverage on the brake grips.

4. If your bike is equipped with toe clips, try pulling up on the pedals, as well as pushing down. This uses different muscles and can give you better efficiency for long rides.

5. When riding a mountain bike on fire trails, it is common to encounter steep downhill sections. To safely deal with these, stop and lower your seat before you descend. This lowers your center of gravity and also allows you to dismount quickly. Raise your seat back to its normal position for uphill sections, to get optimum leverage on the pedals.

6. When riding with a group, it is both safe and polite to regroup periodically. Avoid getting spread out over great distances. It is usually best to have an experienced rider follow in the rear of the group to assist any cyclist having problems.

ABOUT THE AUTHOR

After a career as an electronics engineer, Conrad Boisvert retired in 1990 and began writing. This is his third book on bicycle touring and follows his earlier efforts entitled, *South Bay Bike Trails* and *San Francisco Peninsula Bike Trails,* published in 1990 and 1991, respectively.

Born in New Jersey in 1943, his residence in northern California since 1972 has fulfilled his desire to live where there is a wide variety of readily available outdoor activities. Besides cycling, his interests include tennis, basketball, hiking and skiing. He is the father of three grown children and currently resides in the Willow Glen area of San José.